The curse
of Columbus

The title for this issue is taken from Basil Davidson's *The Story of Africa* (London, Mitchell Beazley, 1984).

© Institute of Race Relations, 1992
ISBN 085001 039 X
Cover design by Arefin & Arefin
Typeset by Spencers (TU), 1-5 Clerkenwell Road, London EC1
Printed by the Russell Press, Gamble Street, Nottingham

RACE & CLASS

A JOURNAL FOR BLACK AND THIRD WORLD LIBERATION

Volume 33   January-March 1992   Number 3

The curse of Columbus

ISSN 0 306 3965

We apologise for the wrong and insensitive use of the term Ulster throughout the article 'Ulster and the downfall of the Labour government 1974-79' in the last issue of *Race & Class*.

Introduction

The Columbian quincentenary is not so much a remembrance of times past as a reconstruction of times present. For, whereas Europe's medieval kings took legitimacy and authority from God's ordinance, the mesh of supra-national and super-powers and transnational conglomerates who arrange our destinies today, need a more sophisticated array of techniques to proclaim the inevitability of current hierarchies of power and the rightfulness of their version of progress. All the more so, when that progress becomes increasingly threatened by the contradictions of its own making.

And what better figure to represent the beneficent unity of the modern world, whether in a Europe that is both integrating and disintegrating at once, or in a US that, riddled with fissures, is yet the hub of a monolithic, global culture, than Columbus? Janus between the medieval and the modern worlds, for those who benefited from the exploitation he opened up, Columbus is the harbinger of progress and prosperity. For those who did not, he is the bringer of catastrophe on an exponential scale.

How mythical indeed is the notion of the linear march of progress, as set in motion by European expansion, is just one of the lessons to be gained from Jan Carew's scholarly and perceptive account of the end of Moorish enlightenment in Spain, and its deliberate extirpation in the cause of racism and bigotry. The backwardness that Spain plunged itself into, even as it initiated the expansion that other imperial nations would profit from, has remained with it to this day, as Matthew Carr demonstrates so eloquently in 'Spain: the Day of the Race'. Ironically, one way that Spain is trying to break through its economic marginalisation is through greater investment – in Latin America.

Carew also shows how the pogroms against the Moors and the Jews in fifteenth- and sixteenth-century Spain foreshadowed the treatment that would be meted out to the indigenous peoples of the Americas. In 'Columbus and the war on indigenous peoples', Michael Stevenson carries this further, elucidating the unparalleled savagery with which European colonisers set about their self-appointed task of 'development' and the ways in which they managed to rationalise and justify, to themselves, their methods.

But Columbus was not just a path to the decimation of the Americas. He was a passage also to the horrors of post-medieval slavery, the rite of passage to the full-blown ideology and practice of modern racism, as Basil Davidson so convincingly argues in 'Columbus: the bones and blood of racism'.

Not that such considerations are allowed to disturb the Columbian myth. Nowhere, for obvious reasons, is it propounded more shrilly and vehemently than in the US, nowhere has it become such a direct political tool in the making of national ideology. The process starts early, as Barbara Ransby shows in her examination of the partial, evasive and distorted way 'Columbus' is dealt with in school textbooks, even the recent ones. And any attempt to redress issues of racism and sexism in education, as well as in the wider social sphere, so as to reflect more fully the (changing) reality of US society, is met with an organised barrage of hostility from the New Right, screaming 'McCarthyism' and 'witch-hunts'. In her biting piece on 'Columbus and the USA: from mythology to ideology', Nancy Murray traces the trajectory of this valediction to democracy.

The Columbian myth as refracted through British eyes is the starting point for Chris Searle's analysis of much of the recent literature – which in itself exemplifies not only some of the ways in which the myth is being resurrected over 1992, but also the resistance to such myth-making and the exposition instead of the realities of racism, exploitation and domination that increasingly characterise the modern world.

Resistance is, of course, at its most vital in Latin America. Tomàs Borge argues that, out of the specific reality of that continent, shaped as it is by a range of different forces, must be generated its own revolutionary development. The uprising in Ecuador, documented here by Lisa Smith, is just one such example – in this instance, of a bitter struggle for land rights and the means of survival which, though ignored by the West, is nonetheless being replicated, in different forms, among different communities across the continent.

Hazel Waters

The record

JAN CAREW

The end of Moorish enlightenment and the beginning of the Columbian era

At the beginning of the Columbian era, thousands of books that the Moors had collected over centuries – priceless masterpieces that their geographers, mathematicians, astronomers, scientists, poets, historians and philosophers had written, and tomes their scholars had translated – were committed to bonfires by priests of the Holy Inquisition. And to cap this atrocity, an estimated three million Moors and 300,000 Jews were expelled from Spain (and this does not include the thousands forced to convert to Catholicism). The burning of thousands of books and the expulsion of the Moors and Jews was a terrible loss to the Renaissance, although this is seldom acknowledged by Eurocentric scholars. And the glaring irony of it all is that the Renaissance would not have been possible without the seminal cultural infusions of Moorish and Jewish scholarship. This had been implanted from the very beginning of Moorish rule in the Iberian peninsula, and by the twelfth and thirteenth centuries had become all-pervasive.

The fall of Granada, on 2 January 1492, marked the end of 800 years of Moorish suzerainty and, 'According to tradition, the valiant General Musa denounced the surrender to the last and rode out of the Elvira Gate never to reappear.'[1] And, on 6 January, four days after the formal surrender, Ferdinand of Aragon and Isabella of Castile rode into the citadel and took the keys of the Alhambra, that marvel of Moorish architecture about which poets and writers had penned jewelled enconiums. Jan Read, who understood the Moorish culture

Jan Carew is Emeritus Professor at Northwestern University, Illinois.

Race & Class, 33, 3 (1992)

better than most, despite the fact she, too, was bent on de-
Africanising it, describes it thus:

> Together with the hanging gardens of the Generalife above, it is
> perhaps the most successful fusion of architecture and landscape
> ever achieved by man . . . Perhaps we can leave the last word to the
> Emperor Charles V as he looked out from a balcony of the Hall of
> the Ambassadors to the heights of the Albaicín opposite and the
> smiling *vega* with its groves and gardens far below. 'Ill-fated', he
> exclaimed, 'is the man who lost all this!'[2]

The young caliph, Abu 'Abdi-Llah ('Boabdil' to the Spaniards),
handed over the keys to the Spanish sovereigns and so, the *Reconquista* (the wresting of Spain from its Moorish conquerors) came to a
dramatic end. Along with the keys to the citadel, there were priceless
tomes and manuscripts which would be scattered and committed to
the flames. Boabdil had surrendered this last Moorish outpost without
a fight to the end, and his dark-skinned and indomitable mother,
'A'isha, had reproached him bitterly saying, 'Weep like a woman for
what you could not defend like a man.'[3]

Under the terms of capitulation, the conquered Moors

> would retain their own customs and religious freedoms and would
> be held accountable only to their own judges . . . [and] Christian
> women married to Moors and others who had converted to Islam
> from Christianity would not be reconverted against their will.[4]

However, a decade later, Isabella, whose religious zealotry and
greed for confiscated Moorish and Jewish property outstripped
Ferdinand's, abrogated this agreement. It was Isabella, too, who
appointed the infamous Spanish Dominican, Tomas de Torquemada,
as Inquisitor-General. She also signed the edict ordering the expulsion
of Jews on 31 March 1492, so that all four of Columbus's voyages were
financed with funds seized from dispossessed Jews. From the moment
the ink had dried on Isabella's edict expelling Moors and Jews and
confiscating their property, ethnocide was to become an intrinsic part
of Spanish domestic and overseas policy. This nefarious edict would
also become the prelude to the extermination of the Guanches of the
Canary Islands (Spain's first overseas territory) and the Tainos, Caribs
and other Native Americans of the New World. This Spanish pre-
cedent established a tradition of conquest and ethnocide that was soon
adopted by all of the European colonisers who came in Spain's
wake.

The thousands of volumes committed to the flames by officials and
agents of the Holy Inquisition at the end of the *Reconquista* embodied
the cream of Islamic and Hellenistic learning, which had been fed
from its earliest beginnings by African roots buried deep in the

creative soil of that much maligned and deliberately misunderstood continent.

At the height of the Moors' rule, the cities they created – like Seville, Córdoba, Toledo, Granada and others – compared to those in Christian-dominated principalities, were centres of unbelievable en-lightenment. At a time when the most insignificant provinces of Moorish Spain contained libraries running into thousands of volumes, the cathedrals, monasteries and palaces of León, under Christian rule, numbered books only by the dozen. For, unlike their Christian counterparts, Moorish rulers

> were often philosophers, mathematicians or poets [and] . . . at a period when [historian] Ibn-Hayyan of Córdoba could write a history of Spain in ten volumes, lively, detailed and well-observed, all that eleventh-century León could offer were the fifteen sparse and imprecise pages of Sampiro, notary to Alfonso V. [5]

In fact, the paltry number of texts the Christians did possess were almost all devotional or liturgical.[6] It was little wonder, then, that in 1492,

> less than twenty years after the introduction of printing in Spain, Elio Antonio de Nebrija, historiographer royal to Queen Isabella, published in Salamanca a grammar of the Castilian language, the first such work ever compiled for a European vernacular . . .
> 'What is this for?' Isabella is said to have asked . . . when Nebrija's book was presented to her by a royal courtier.
> 'Your Majesty,' the courtier is reported to have answered, 'language is always the companion of empire.'[7]

But the Moors had already known this for centuries. Arabic grammars had had to be created so that language could be the companion of an Islamic empire stretching across three continents.[8]

On 12 October 1492, eight months after the fall of Granada, Columbus landed on the beaches of the Taino island of Guanahani. Thus, Spain claimed that it had discovered a 'new world', and it embarked upon a shameful course of ethnocide against indigenous peoples of the Americas that made its atrocities against the conquered Moors, Jews and Guanches pale by comparison.

Coming to the Iberian peninsula in the wake of the Vandals and Visigoths, the Moors had, over their long tenure, civilised the land they called 'al-Andalus', a name which derived from the former designation of the Iberian peninsula as the 'Land of the Vandals'. But once the *Reconquista* had ended, a unified Spain seemed bent on moving backwards into the future. With the end of Moorish power, the Spanish not only went on a book-burning spree, they also tried to erase every vestige of Moorish cultural influence from their consciousness. The Holy Inquisition, with its *limpieza de sangre* (cleansing of the [Spanish] blood), its zealotry and its all-encompassing and repressive tentacles reaching into the lives of the highest and lowliest in the land, set about de-civilising the Iberian peninsula. And the persecution was most wrenching in the lives of Spain's principal culture-bringers: the Moors and the Jews. But the Moors, who were more numerous and who were expelled later than the Jews, resisted long after the fall of Granada. Jan Read recounts:

> In 1568 a second and even more violent rebellion broke out in the Alpujarras. Its leader, Fernando de Valor (Maulvi 'Abd-Allah Mohammad ibn-Umayya), justified his action by declaring, 'We are in Spain and we have ruled this land for nine hundred years . . . We are no band of thieves but a kingdom; nor is Spain less abandoned to vices than was Rome.'[9]

This particular rebellion was so serious that Phillip II had to call on help from Don Juan of Austria to put it down.

But in talking of the Moors and Jews in the context of that transitional period between the rise of Spanish power and the final defeat of the former and the expulsion of both, it must be remembered that neither the terms 'Moor' nor 'Jew' referred to a uniform racial type. They were both the products of polyglot racial mixtures in North Africa and Spain, and only their cultural and religious trappings would have enabled an outsider to distinguish one from the other.

During their long tenure as rulers, 'The Moors . . . had set a pattern of peaceful symbiosis in their tolerant treatment of Christians and Jews; and a new class analogous to the Mozarabs [Christians under Muslim rule] was to appear: the Mudejars, or Muslims living under Christian rule.[10]

For centuries, Muslims, Christians and Jews had lived side-by-side, and, in many instances, had so intermarried that numerous families were part Muslim, part Christian and part Jew. The teachings of the Prophet, too, had stressed repeatedly that peoples of all races and colours were equal in the sight of Allah, and these teachings were not only preached but practised.

The persecution of Moors and Jews, therefore, and their tragic and inhuman expulsion, gave added momentum to the process of de-civilisation and the institutionalisation of racism in Christian Spain after the *Reconquista*. And this peculiarly European phenomenon of a manicheistic racism (white against black and brown) wove itself into the fabric of Christianity and remains embedded there to this day.

At its zenith, Muslim power stretched from China, across the Himalayas into India, through the Middle East, and deep into the Nile valley. It criss-crossed all of North Africa, reached down to Dar-es-Salaam in East Africa and went as far south as Ghana in West Africa.

And it then spread north across the Pillars of Hercules to stretch from Portugal's Atlantic coast, through the Iberian peninsula, over the Pyrenees, into France's Rhone valley and north along the Biscay coast to Tours.

This vast and complex Islamic geo-political, cultural and racial spread is almost invariably viewed through a spectrum of religious intolerance and racial chauvinism by Eurocentric scholars. Even the words used to describe other peoples, their religion and their culture underscore a continual struggle by Europe to come to terms with their biased racial perceptions. Words such as 'Islam' and 'Islamic', or 'Muslim' (as noun) and 'Muslim' (adjective) have been thrown about without a sense of their particular contextual significance. 'Islam', the noun, refers to the religion begun by Muhammad in the sixth century. 'Islamic', the adjective, refers to the particular character of the religion, which then reflects on the noun that follows, as in 'Islamic calendar'. 'Muslim', the noun, refers to a person who is an adherent of Islam, and 'Muslim', the adjective which derives from the noun, refers to the particular character of a Muslim and, variously, to the civilisation of Islam. The distinction between the two is now blurred, with common usage offering one clues as to where a particular term should or should not be used.

The terms 'Arab', 'Berber', 'Moor', 'Sanhaja tribes' and 'Tuareg' have also undergone several permutations. These terms are ethno-geographical, rather than religio-cultural in origin. 'Arab' originally referred to an inhabitant of the Arabian peninsula who spoke Arabic. But recent research has pointed to the fact that 'Arabia was the oldest Ethiopian colony', that 'the Cushites were the original Arabians' and that 'Ancient literature assigns their first settlement to the extreme southwestern point of the peninsula. From thence they spread northward and eastward over Yemen, Hadramaut and Oman.'[11]

When the 'Arabs', therefore, began to spread westwards into Egypt and across the Red Sea, they were largely absorbed into the black and brown gene pools of the peoples of the Nile, the Sahara and the northern Mediterranean and Middle Eastern colonies scattered across the northern rim of Africa. As W.E.B. Du Bois pointed out, 'The term Arab is applied to any people professing Islam . . . much race mixing has occurred so that while the term has a cultural value, it is of little ethnic significance and is often misleading.' Furthermore, not all Arabs were, or are, Muslims; nor, for that matter, were, or are, all Muslims, Arabs. It is likely though, that those with whom Europe dealt in the period of the Muslim presence in Spain were. On the other hand, all 'Moors', that is persons originating in Morocco, and 'Berbers', again a very imprecise term referring to polyglot Saharan white, black and brown North African groups of largely nomadic people, were officially Muslim. They were converted to Islam in the sweep of the religion across northern Africa between 640 and 700. And while they had some Arab admixture after their long period of cohabitation, they were primarily African. Arabs, Berbers, Tuaregs and Moors of every possible shade and colour were present in that invading army that conquered Spain, but it was the Moors, who, coming in successive waves for eight centuries, left a permanent imprint upon the Spanish language and culture in particular, and European civilisation in general.

For European scholars, the historical mileposts in Europe's relationship with the Arabs, the Saracens and the Moors were the Crusades, the fall of Constantinople to the Turks and the fall of Granada to the Catholic rulers of Spain. These events are locked in a time-warp which, in turn, has created a tunnel vision of history, with a demonised image of the Muslim as an infidel and a perpetual enemy of the 'devout' Christian. And in this racist mythology, even bandits like el Cid are practically deified as soldiers of the Cross fighting against Muslim 'barbarians'. We are not told that, after his string of victories (as a clever field commander, he had devised effective methods for overcoming the advantage of the Almoravid's massed infantry), he time and time again joined forces with Muslim groups opposed to the Almoravids. In the wake of el Cid's premature death, however, the Almoravids reconquered the whole of southern Spain and Portugal and inflicted a crushing defeat on Alfonso VI, his erstwhile mentor. Thus, the victories of this legendary Spanish hero, who had fought first as a mercenary and then as a usurper, were brought to naught by Moorish conquerors. But Spanish and other European historians have, over the centuries, developed a case of amnesia when dealing with this sequel to el Cid's victories.

At the same time, however, some Arab/Islamic scholars, while deriding the narrow focus of the Eurocentric tunnel vision, and the implicit racism built into it against them, become racists themselves when dealing with black Africans. In addition to the reprehensible role they played in the slave trade, they have developed a myopic and chauvinistic vision of their role in history, and cling to Greek and Middle Eastern civilisations while ignoring the tremendous contribution that Africa made to Islamic civilisation. When the Prophet Muhammad fled to Medina, some of his most devoted followers crossed the Red Sea and began to proselytise in Ethiopia. So, the first significant groups of the converted were Africans. The Muslim religion, therefore, was filtered through the great African civilisations of the Nile valley – the Ethiopian, the Nubian and the Egyptian – in its early stages. These ancient civilisations provided Islam with an intellectual, cultural and spiritual nexus from which its message and its innermost content would be immeasurably humanised and enriched.

Four centuries after Islam had taken root in Africa, and the

Islamic empire was at its zenith, the Almoravids, a Sanhaja extension of the Tuareg people,[12] carried Islamic/Moorish culture victoriously into Europe in 1086, 'giving new life to Muslim al-Andalus'.[13] In fact, the predominantly midnight-black Almoravids, as relatively new converts to Islam, were the most ardent in demanding that those in authority should once more adhere strictly to the tenets of morality and justice that were laid down in the *Holy Koran*. These new devotees (the Almoravids), at first intolerant of the urbane and decadent intellectuals and scholars in the cities they conquered, were, however, eventually corrupted by these very intellectuals. Their pristine energy, though, did manage to impregnate Moorish literature, art, music and philosophy with new rhythms of life and a heightened sense of being. Their musicians, storytellers, griots and catechists popularised their religious and cultural message with a fervour that the original Moorish conquerors had lost. And they did this by reaching into the reservoir of African oral traditions, which were so ancient that seers and griots had declared that these primordial traditions had first come to them 'from the breath of God'.

Biased historians, however, tend to portray the Almoravids (the dark Moors) as bigots; while uncouth European marauders like the Crusaders, waving Christian banners across the Middle East, are depicted as pious soldiers of Christ. There is an instinctive and deep-seated reluctance on the part of Eurocentric historians to acknowledge the Moors as the bringers of cultural and scientific enlightenment to Europe. And when they are compelled to make grudging acknowledgements of this fact, they proceed to 'whiten' the Moors, to tear them away from any suggestion of having black African roots. But the stubborn fact remains that, at the height of its power, the Moorish empire in Africa stretched from the western half of Algeria through Morocco and as far south as Ghana; while, in Europe, this empire extended itself from the Atlantic coast, across the Pyrenees to the Rhone valley and parallel to the Biscayan littoral as far north as Tours. And now, five centuries after the fall of Granada, the rainbow array of colours and racial types seen in the faces of the contemporary population of Morocco – from blond and blue-eyed, through various shades of brown to anthracite black – is not all that different from what it was in the Moorish empire in the eleventh century, despite new racial infusions by migrants and successive waves of settlers.

Is it any wonder, then, that scholars, blinkered by their racism, have difficulty acknowledging who the Almoravids (1056-1147) really were; or that they continue to describe them variously as 'descended from the Sanhaja tribes [sic] of the Sahara'[14] or 'the desert Sanhaja from whom the Almoravids had first drawn support',[15] suggesting that the Almoravids, themselves, were something else and that they got the Sanhaja to help in their campaign; or as 'the African troops, the Sinhaja';[16] or as a 'powerful Berber Sanhajah tribe [sic]'.[17] Eurocentric historians continue to produce 'learned' treatises on 'fierce' and 'warlike' Saharan 'tribes' like the Sanhajas, Berbers, Tuaregs, etc. – 'fierce' and 'warlike' being euphemisms for 'simple-minded and blood-thirsty'. Somehow, the most blood-thirsty and murderous of European adventurers are never described as being 'fierce' or 'warlike'.

Evidence of the Moors' civilising mission is strewn across the Iberian peninsula. It is, in fact, because of the Moorish conquest and the Moorish civilising mission that the factional European tribes and kingdoms were able to direct their energies from fighting amongst themselves to studying the very philosophies and sciences that would propel them out of their insular perspectives into uncharted seas and across new continents of the imagination.

Although there were many instances wherein some prized Arabic texts were translated into Latin and/or Romance languages and the originals destroyed, Christian Spain carried out a systematic anti-Moorish programme after the *Reconquista*. Though benefiting greatly from the scientific, the philosophical and the literary innovations brought to them by the Moors, the Spanish and other Europeans systematically wiped out any and all reference to the great influence that the Moors had on their subsequent development.

The Arabs brought the works of classical Greek thinkers back to Europe by translating, synthesising and improving upon them. Unlike Christian theologians, who forbade scholars from considering ideas outside the prescribed ecclesiastical canons of the day (Galileo and Hus fell foul of these restrictions), Islam accommodated new ideas with grace and a civilised tolerance. Moorish scholars believed that there were fundamental links between mathematics and religion. They conceived of the universe as an entity which God kept recreating at every moment of existence, as being dynamic rather than static, and this dynamic quality was brought out very effectively in Moorish mathematics. They therefore saw science not as a denial, but as an affirmation, of faith.

Arab scholars had found a particular fascination in the philosophy and science of the early Greeks and, after translating the texts of Aristotle, Plato, Ptolemy, Euclid, Heracleitus, Galen, Hippocrates and others, they analysed and improved upon them, drawing from their wide-ranging intellectual experiences and observations in the vast territories they ruled, and the polyglot races and peoples with whom they traded in knowledge, ideas and goods. Arab and Moorish scholars not only absorbed and synthesised the knowledge of the Ethiopians, the Nubians, the Egyptians, the Jews, the Phoenicians, the Greeks, the Chinese, the Persians and the Indians, they also used an innovative scientific method that their genius had devised to transform theory into practice. This new and momentous forward leap in the theoretical and applied sciences evidenced itself in Moorish mathematics, medicine, astronomy, navigation and new concepts of world geography and philosophy. The popularity of Moorish scholarship was such that, for centuries, Arabic was commonly accepted as the language of scholars from Europe, Asia and Africa, and the Moorish intellectual centres in Toledo, Córdova, Seville and Granada became Meccas of learning. For centuries, too, the rulers of Europe, and their wealthiest courtiers and merchant princes, relied on Moorish physicians and surgeons to cure them of their various ailments. And they judged those roving medical specialists by their skills and not their colour. Even after the *Reconquista*, Christian rulers continued surreptitiously to invite Moorish scholars to their kingdoms, because of a profound respect for their knowledge and expertise.

Moorish scientific and organisational abilities transformed their cities into extraordinarily advanced urban centres. Not only were their public and private buildings aesthetically pleasing, their architects and planners created cities the likes of which had never previously been seen in Europe. Some historians assert that the Moors of Spain, unlike their nomadic kith and kin from the desert kingdoms, were essentially an urban people. But this statement is only a half-truth, and needs to be qualified and expanded upon, for cities require a countryside capable of feeding large populations.

The Moors had been able to create a harmony in the rhythms of life in the city and in the countryside. They dotted the map of al-Andalus with their cities and towns, but they could only do this because the surrounding countryside was kept fertile and productive – with advanced drainage and irrigation systems, reservoirs, aqueducts, sophisticated storage facilities and efficient marketing, transportation and trading networks. The Moors also brought the countryside into their cities with fantastic gardens, parks, lush inner courtyards and a constant supply of pure water. The gardens in Moorish cities, both public and private, were known as 'paradises', a fitting term to describe those exquisite botanical marvels.

Different Moorish cities came to be known for their particular forte – Córdova for its libraries and collections, Seville for its music and musical instruments and Toledo as a centre of industry and learning – but all shared a common feature of highly sophisticated urban management and unbroken and seminal connections with the land. Moorish cities were noted for their public hospitals, public baths, lighted thoroughfares, hot and cold running water, magnificent religious monuments, the grandeur of their mosques, gardens with exotic plants and even more exotic birds, and beautifully designed fountains.

Ibn Khaldun (1332-1406), a towering African genius, published a seven-volume history of the world, entitled *The Book of Examples and Collections from the Early and Subsequent Information Concerning the Days of Arabs, Non-Arabs, and Berbers.*[18] Ibn Khaldun was the first to develop the theory of the cyclical development of society, wherein a given society flourishes for a time and then declines under the weight of pomp, luxury and growing inefficiency. It was Ibn Khaldun who suggested that 'the ideal framework for Islamic life is a holy city with a nomadic periphery, with the city representing the stronghold of learning and meditation and the nomadic hinterland guaranteeing the constant influx of fresh elements [people unspoiled by urban culture]'.[20] Not only a historian, Ibn Khaldun fathered the sciences of economics, anthropology, political science and urban planning, and his erudition was such that, up to the present time, his birthday is celebrated by Islamic and non-Islamic scholars all over the world. In his lucid and persuasive writings, he formulated systems of city planning and dealt with problems of 'air pollution, physical layout, zoning, education, and city support for arts and sciences'.[20]

Moorish sanitary engineers, city planners, doctors and public health officials understood that high public health standards could only be achieved when there was an educated and responsible citizenry. A great deal of attention, therefore, was paid to inculcating the idea that effective public health began with good individual habits of personal hygiene by rich and poor alike. The smallest Moorish villages, hamlets and towns had public baths. As the *Reconquista* progressed, however, benighted Catholic priests had the public baths closed and the faithful were told that daily ablutions were sinful. In 1568, Phillip II 'banned public baths until then found in the smallest of Moorish towns and villages', thus 'delivering a body blow to Muslim tradition'.[21]

A succession of plagues and famines fell upon both the Spanish cities and the countryside as the *Reconquista* progressed and the Moors were driven out. The countryside was then denuded of food products and vast acreages were reserved for sheep and cattle rearing or left idle and uncultivated. The plagues that savaged Spanish and other European cities in the century after Columbus's first voyage were given ample opportunity to go on the rampage amongst populations encouraged by their prelates to live by the adage that 'filthiness was next to godliness'. Paradoxically, European historians blame these plagues on the syphilis that Spanish males allegedly caught from Taino women. But blaming the victim, especially when ethnocide has ensured that the victim cannot speak back, is an intellectually dishonest pastime in which Eurocentric historians have indulged for centuries. As Richard Ford, a perceptive scholar tells us:

Ablution and lustral purification formed an article of faith with the Jew and Moslem, with whom 'cleanliness is godliness' . . . Ximenez [who afterwards became a Cardinal] . . . a shirtless Franciscan, induced Ferdinand and Isabella, at the conquest of Granada, to close and abolish the Moorish baths [and] . . . Fire, not water, became the grand element of inquisitorial purification.[22]

Even their most implacable Spanish enemies acknowledged that the Moors were superb agricultural scientists, for they had not only cultivated the fertile areas, but also brought the arts of 'dry farming' to the high, bleak mesas, and reconstructed and improved the old Roman irrigation systems and introduced a variety of new crops like cereals, beans and peas of various types, olives, almonds and vines – invaluable sources of protein and other indispensable nutrients. Here, for example, is an entry made by a Moorish official in March 961,

Fig trees are grafted in the manner called Tarqi: the winter corn grows up; and most of the fig trees break into leaf . . . the falcons of Valencia lay eggs . . . Sugar cane is planted. The first roses and lilies appear. In kitchen gardens, the beans begin to shoot.[23]

Other crops introduced by the Moors included a variety of herbs, the orange (which was first grown in Valencia, hence the term Valencia orange), pomegranates, bananas, coconuts, maize and rice. Take, for example, this poem by Mahbub the Grammarian, an eleventh century poet, eulogising a great water-wheel in motion. These water-wheels, which were introduced by the Moors, were invaluable sources of energy for irrigation, the grinding of grain, etc.

She sobs and weeps her streams of sparkling water,
She weeps, and the garden smiles with many a petal
Of deepest red, of white and brilliant yellow;
You'd say the smith made scoops of pearl, and not of metal.[24]

The Moors had a respect for nature that bordered on idolatry, while the Spanish felt that nature was impregnated with hidden, antagonistic forces that had to be conquered and exploited. The cosmology which conceived of nature and all natural forces as being 'threatening' was an intrinsic part of the Church's teachings. Forests were invariably depicted as being dark and menacing, the home of wild beasts and evil spirits. Conversely, in the Moorish cosmology, the forest was a place of light and enchantment. As the *Reconquista* progressed, the Moors' love and respect for their environment was increasingly depicted by their Spanish conquerors as evidence of their being heretics, pagans and infidels. Centuries later, Garcia Lorca resurrected the creative vision of the Moors and gypsies of Andalusia in his poetry and plays. When he wrote about 'the forests of my flesh', he showed a profound understanding of the forgotten Moorish belief that forests were, in fact, the 'lungs' of the earth.

At the zenith of Moorish power, al-Andalus, that land of many cities, attracted scholars from England, France, Germany, Italy and the rest of Europe, as well as from distant parts of the Muslim empire. After the Mongol conquests, too, al-Andalus benefited from the intellectual cross-fertilisation of Muslim scholars fleeing from the wrath of Ghengis Khan and his descendants.

Many of the European scholars came to learn Arabic so that they could read and popularise the knowledge acquired in Moorish centres of learning amongst their own relatively backward people. The Moorish city of Toledo, which was reconquered in 1085, became a cornucopia of newly discovered learning for a benighted population of Europe beyond the Pyrenees, and Christian rulers, from Alphonso VII (1126-57) onward, encouraged the establishment of schools of translation and of Arabic/Oriental studies in order to ensure a steady flow of new scholarship into their kingdoms.

It is intriguing that, on the one hand, there have been the racist and bigoted religious slanders directed at the Moors after the fall of Granada in 1492, while, on the other, two centuries earlier, European scholars had developed an insatiable appetite for Arabic works in mathematics, astronomy, physics, alchemy, medicine, geography other natural sciences, and philosophy, not to speak of literature and music. Both Thomas Aquinas (1225-74) and Dante (1265-1321), for example, were virulently anti-Islam and anti-Arab. Aquinas, however, constantly referred to Arab scholars and Arab thought with a profound respect, and Dante chose to put Muslim scholars, such as Salah al-Din, Ibn Sina (Avicenna) and Ibn Rushd (Averroës), among the great thinkers of antiquity in his *Divine Comedy*.[25]

The great Arab philosopher Ibn Rushd (known as 'Averroës' in Europe) had perhaps the most widely acknowledged and profound effect on western thought. Born and reared in Córdova in 1126, at the time of the Almoravids (the dark-skinned, Saharan Moors), Averroës was best known for his translations of Aristotle. His name became so closely linked with Aristotelian philosophy that whole schools of philosophy were set up in Paris, Padua and Bologna to spread 'Averroism'.[26] Besides philosophy, he was also extremely influential as a purveyor of new medical knowledge. In fact, Averroës was a renaissance scholar long before the Renaissance: he was a poet, scientist, philosopher, historian and mathematician.

But Averroës might very well have lived and died in obscurity if it were not for two fortuitous circumstances: the patronage of the enlightened Moorish ruler Abu Ya'qub Yusuf and the enthusiastic support of the Spanish Jewish philosopher Musa Ibn Maymun (1135-1204) (also known as Maimonides).[27] Thanks to Abu Ya'qub

Yusuf, Averroës work was published in thirty-eight volumes. And thanks to the Spanish Jews – in particular, Maimonides, who, like Averroës, was born in Córdova – the first school of Averroism was established. The impact of Averroës' philosophies was such that they continued to provoke debate throughout Europe for several centuries after his death.

Much later, Cervantes, living astride the sixteenth and seventeenth centuries, the Spanish 'Golden Age', would die in poverty because of indifferent patrons. Despite his monumental contribution to the Spanish language, literature and culture, Cervantes was ignored by philistine aristocrats like the Archbishop of Toledo, the Count of Lemos and the Duke of Bejar, whose patronage he had sought in vain. By contrast, during the succession of 'golden ages' that Islam had inspired, geniuses like Africans Ziryab and Ibn Khaldun and the Moorish Averroës, had unlimited resources placed at their disposal and were acclaimed and revered by highly educated and enlightened rulers.

There can be no denying the fact that Moorish scholarship, and Moorish culture as a whole, had an intellectual ripple-effect on Europe. They moved in concentric rings from centres of learning to the most backward areas of the continent. Their geographers and mathematicians measured global distances accurately for the first time. Without the improved Moorish/Arab astrolabe, the lateen sail and the advances made by Arabs in navigation, astronomy and the nautical sciences in general, the idea of sailing west to reach the Indies would never have crystallised in a mind trapped in the thraldom of medieval superstition, as Columbus's was when he first set out from his lowly birthplace outside Genoa.

It is ironic, that, to this day, five centuries after Columbus's first voyage, and four-and-a-half since the Tainos and Caribs were exterminated, the Spanish in their homeland, and the *mestizo* (Hispanic, African and Amerindian racial mixtures) ruling elements in Latin America, continue to make derisory noises about the 'purity of their blood' in order to banish unconscious memories of ineradicable Moorish/Jewish/African cultural and racial infusions. Regardless of skin colour and feature, they are forever ready to choose the Visigoths as ancestors rather than the dark-skinned and civilised Moors. And today, the legacy of ethnocide that Columbus left five centuries ago, is still with us in Guatemala, Honduras, Panama, Venezuela, Colombia, Peru, Ecuador, Bolivia, Chile, Paraguay and Brazil.

In the midst of the neo-Creationist 1992 quincentennial festivities, we should re-examine the Columbus legacy and make sure that we are commemorating the epic struggles of those who fought to humanise the Americas, and not celebrating those who sought to make ethnocide, racism, slavery and greed intrinsic to our American heritage.

References

1   Jan Read, *The Moors in Spain and Portugal* (Totowa, NJ, Rowman and Littlefield, 1975), p. 217.
2   Read, op. cit., p. 201.
3   Read, op. cit., p. 219.
4   Read, op. cit., p. 218.
5   Ibid., p. 100.
6   Ibid.
7   Kirkpatrick Sale, *The Conquest of Paradise* (New York, 1990), p. 18.
8   The Arabic names and words are taken from various sources, many of which do not use the same phonetic representation for similar words. Written Arabic uses only consonants and the vowels must then be surmised from the context. This applies as well to some consonants, such as the hard 'g', 'q', and 'k', which are frequently used to represent the same sound.
9   Read, op. cit., p. 224.
10   Ibid.
11   Wayne B. Chandler, 'The Moor: light of Europe's Dark Age', in Van Sertima (ed.), *The African Presence in Early Europe* (New Brunswick, NJ, Transaction Books, 1985), p. 151.
12   Chandler, op. cit., p. 152.
13   Anwar G. Chejne, *Muslim Spain: its history and culture* (Minneapolis, University of Minnesota Press, 1974), p. 78.
14   Read, op. cit., 124.
15   Ibid., p. 163.
16   Titus Burchhardt, *Moorish Culture in Spain* (New York, McGraw-Hill, 1972), p. 124.
17   Chejne, op. cit., p. 69.
18   Ibid., p. 274.
19   M.A. Martin, 'Abd ar-Rahman bin Muhammad bin Khaldun', in John R. Hayes (ed.), *The Genius of Arab Civilisation* (Cambridge, Mass., MIT Press, 1978), p. 73.
20   Martin, op. cit., p. 73.
21   Read, op. cit., p. 234.
22   Read, Ibid.
23   Read, op. cit., pp. 80-81.
24   Ibid., p. 82.
25   Chejne, op. cit., pp. 404-5.
26   Read, op. cit., pp. 187-9.
27   Chejne, op. cit., pp. 329-33.

BASIL DAVIDSON

Columbus: the bones and blood of racism

The man himself seems to have been driven by an overweening
personal ambition and a truly monstrous greed, as strange and violent
in character as the ends he sought and the adventures he invited. His
cautious biographer in the *Encyclopaedia Britannica* explains that the
'discoverer' of the Caribbean possessed a mind that was 'lofty and
imaginative, and so taut that his actions, thoughts and writings do at
times suggest a man just this side of the edge of insanity'. But not,
perhaps, so very far 'this side', while in behaviour this Cristóbal
Colón, as he usually called himself (being in any case of dubious
Genoese extraction), may stand in history as a worthy leader of the
plunderers and tyrants who hastened to follow him across the seas. All
this is well known, even while one need not be surprised that the five
hundredth anniversary of his initial voyage should have become an
occasion for rejoicing in some parts of the Americas. Here I want to
look 'behind Columbus' at what our world today may more widely
regard as his greatest achievement: his first opening of a 'New World'
to be 'developed' by the merciless use of chattel slaves.

Chattel slavery has to be seen from the start as inseparable from the
Columbus project, and certainly in Columbus's own mind. He himself
insisted that it was. 'He raised crosses everywhere', recalls his encyclo-
paedic biographer, 'but he kept his eye on the material value of things
even to the extent of seeing men as goods for sale.' He lost little time,
moreover, in getting into the business of sending Caribbean

*Basil Davidson is an anti-imperialist scholar and writer who has campaigned for African
liberation for many years. Among his more recent books are 'No fist is big enough to
hide the sky': the liberation of Guiné and Cape Verde (London, Zed, 1981) and The Story
of Africa (London, Mitchell Beazley, 1984).*

Race & Class, 33, 3, (1992)

captives back for sale in Spain. The dates on the calendar tell the essential story and deploy its ferocious implications. Aside from the enslavement of Caribbean peoples, the enslavement of imported Africans in the Caribbean, and soon elsewhere, was in full swing within a dozen years or so. The Spanish government's earliest proclamation of laws concerned with the export of enslaved captives to the other side of the ocean – mainly, at this date, to the island of Hispaniola (Haiti and San Domingo) – came as early as 1501, only nine years after Columbus's first voyage. Some of these earliest victims were white: but already how many were black – were African – may be glimpsed in a complaint of 1503 sent back to Spain by the governor of Hispaniola, Ovando. He told the Crown that fugitive 'Negro' slaves were teaching disobedience to the 'Indians', and could not be recaptured. It would, therefore, be wise for the Crown to desist from sending African captives: they would only add to troubles already great enough. But the Crown, naturally, did no such thing. Even by now, there was too much money at stake.

These early slaves, like others later on, proved incurably rebellious. Huge African revolts shook island after island, and the records are copiously eloquent on the incapacity of settlers and garrisons to put them down. Never mind, the project set moving by Columbus continued to prosper. In 1515, there came the first shipment of slave-grown West Indian sugar back to Spain, and three years later, another date to be remembered, the first cargo of captives from Africa to be shipped to the West Indies, not by way of Spain or Portugal (then under the same Crown), but directly from an African port of embarcation. With this, the long-enduring and hugely profitable 'triangular trade' had its inception: trade-goods from Europe to Africa for the purchase of captives from African merchants; purchased captives sold into enslavement across the ocean; and sugar (chiefly sugar) back to Europe. Such was the potent value of this trade that millions of African captives would be despatched along that *via dolorosa*, and centuries would pass before it could be stopped.

In this perspective, then, Columbus was the father of the slave trade to the Americas; and this trade, far more than any other consequence attached to his name, may be seen – it seems to me without the least manipulating of the evidence – as composing the true and enduring curse of Columbus. Should Columbus then be seen, as well, as the father of the racism which was to excuse or justify this massive work of enslavement? Was this racism of the slave trade in any case a new thing, or was it simply an elaboration of earlier justifications for medieval forms of bondage? When can one say, with some solidity of judgement, that racism in the modern sense – the plain and directly instrumental sense of crude exploitation – actually began? The argument here is that it began with the early consequences of Columbus.

Slavery was nothing new, of course, in Europe; far from it. In medieval Europe, it had long depended on supplies of captives from pre-Christian Slav lands and then from Muslim lands in northern Africa or further east; and, at least in Mediterranean Europe, a trade in captives was both permanent and pervasive. Papal prohibitions on the enslaving of Christians made little difference, and the Genoese were not the only Europeans in the business to shrug off excommunication for persisting in the trade of selling Christians. It remains that none of this slavery was chattel slavery, mass slavery, plantation slavery: rather did it take the form of what may perhaps be called 'wageless labour' – coerced, but in no way subject to any kind of 'market law'. Slaves were bought and sold after their capture, and prices varied with the times; but a market in wages had still to come into existence. Demand was overwhelmingly for domestic labour of one kind or another and, in general, only the rich and privileged could afford to buy and maintain this labour. This was a slavery that could involve great pain and misery, but rather seldom was it a hopeless Calvary: the relatively high cost of slaves helped to limit the persecutions they were otherwise liable to suffer.

The point is worth emphasis. Throughout the High Middle Ages (roughly, the tenth through the thirteenth centuries), in Goitein's authoritative summary, slavery 'was neither industrial nor agricultural. With the exception of the armies, which were largely composed of mercenaries who were legally slaves, it was not collective but individual. It was a personal service in the widest sense of the word, which, when the master served was of high rank or wealthy, carried with it great economic advantages as well as social prestige . . . In and out of bondage, the slave was a member of the family.'[1] No doubt there were exceptions, but I am not concerned with exceptions here; I am concerned with the general run of things. I have read quite a few accounts of plantation slavery in the Caribbean, most lately the horrible and revolting memoirs of Thomas Thistlewood; and I have found in them nothing that remotely resembles the domestic slavery of medieval times.

If that was the general situation in lands round the Mediterranean, it was just as true of tropical African lands further south. Absorbed into extended-family structures, slaves in Africa – and, here again, the records are copious and unequivocal – could expect with a fair confidence to accede to full family rights without long delay. They could marry into their owner's families. They could inherit their owner's wealth. They could make careers in the public service; and wherever slaves acquired military training, armaments, and corresponding disciplines or connexions, they could (and quite often did) seize state power, govern as kings, and even found dynasties of kings. I am not here putting in a good word for slavery, any more than for dynasties of kings. I am only emphasising the differences between modes of enslavement. Not surprisingly, these different modes gave rise to different ways of thinking about slaves: to different ideologies, as the schoolmen would say.

In Spain and Portugal, for example, there was also a large number of slaves before the New World was discovered by Columbus. But there were very few chattel slaves, and no sensible owner would have considered that his or her slaves were of a naturally and inherently inferior kind of human being. There was, in short, no ideology of instrumentalist racism. By the fifteenth century, most such slaves in Iberia were from North Africa. They lived hard lives, and yet, so far as the evidence goes, a good deal less hard than the 'free workers' who toiled alongside them. 'Slaves – as all servants – of wealthy and powerful men were [in those times] better off materially, and before the courts, than were free labourers. If their work was not domestic' – tied to the home, that is – 'they might travel the country or live apart from their masters'; sometimes they could benefit, if they wished (and it is not at all clear that many would have wished), from early manumission.[2] The point here, may I be allowed to insist, is that this was a servitude, however much otherwise to be deplored, which did not foster, because it did not have to foster, the ideology that slaves were slaves because they belonged to an inherently inferior humanity: to a humanity, as it was going to develop in the mentality of the slave trade, that could be 'set apart' as being barely human at all. To grasp the nature of the medieval relationship of bondage, as it appears generally to have been, one can usefully study the medieval iconography of slaves, including slaves from Africa. They are seen and shown as servants like other servants: but valuable servants, costly servants, even cherished servants. They were no more inherently inferior than they were easily expendable.[3]

*   *   *

Was there, then, no racism before the major onset of the Atlantic slave trade? It is a teased issue because the words in general use are vague, but overall the answer is in the negative. There was vast misunderstanding, gross abuse, bewildered superstition. But there was no racism in the instrumentalist sense in which the term is rightly used today. Broadly, in those days when the 'known world' was so very small and narrow, human deviation from the norm was believed to grow with physical distance (yet is it, really, so very different today?). Neighbours were entirely 'normal' and 'non-deviant', even if distrusted or disliked. Near-neighbours might also be fairly normal. But peoples far away began to become exceedingly strange until, as imagined distance widened, they altogether ceased to be human like you and me. The locus classicus of this view of life is probably a passage in the histories of Herodotus (c.450 BC) where, he relates, 'Aristeas, son of Caystrobius, a native of Marmora' in nearby Asia Minor (Turkey today) 'journeyed to the country of the Issedones'. These lived a long way off, but were still reasonably human. Yet 'beyond the Issedones live the one-eyed Arismaspians', clearly deviant in having only one eye apiece, 'and beyond them the griffins who guard the gold'; and the griffins, whatever exactly they may have been, were obviously much more than deviant.[4] So it was, in medieval times, that distant peoples were confidently reported as 'having heads that grow beneath their shoulders', or a single eye in the middle of their chests, or, if they were women – as the Florentine Malfante was reporting back from the central Sahara in 1447 – as being able to produce up to five children at a birth. In those times, when the Earth was so flat that you could risk falling off the edge, anything was possible.

Such beliefs seem to have been universal in one form or another, and they long persisted among peoples beyond the reach of the 'known world'. Less than half a century ago, for instance (but the instances are many), the Lugbara of Uganda (numbering then some 200,000 souls) were found to believe in all good faith that people became hostile, strange, and 'upside-down' in the measure that they dwelt farther away or far from the Lugbara homeland. Of the most distant strangers known to the Lugbara, even if known only by hearsay, there were creatures who habitually walked on their heads or hands, and indulged in other habits which the Lugbara thought perverse and wicked.[5] Distance multiplied deviation; and all this bespoke customary superstition, distrust of foreigners, various on-slaughts of xenophobia and so on. But it did not bespeak racism.

The transition from beliefs such as this to all that superstructure of instrumentalist justification of mass enslavement, of racist enslave-ment, which began with the Columbian voyages was an often complex and contradictory process in the European mind. But it can first be seen at work in the case of the Portuguese, if only because their active involvement in mass enslavement, plantation enslavement, came at least half a century, or even longer, before that of other European peoples (in some degree with the exception of the Spanish). Beginning with the import of a few hundred trans-Saharan captives (mostly Berbers of the desert) in the 1440s, they found a home market which rapidly demanded more. These early African captives were sold on the open Iberian market for the most part as domestic servants who would also, if they revealed a talent for learning and literacy, serve as clerks and trusted commercial agents. Their small numbers of the fifteenth century were merely added to the much larger number already in the country and in Spain; and their arrival called for no rethinking of Portuguese attitudes to the status and condition of slavery.

But all this changed after 1500 and following years, and so did much else. The Earth would soon cease to be flat, the stars no longer hang fixed immutably in space, and even the sun would stop revolving and stand still, until much that yesterday had seemed sacred and un-questionable was due to be thrust aside, forgotten or derided. Ferocious times lay ahead such as even the Middle Ages, with its racks and thumbscrews, had not envisaged; and whole continents would feel their impact and bleed from their destructions. This is the context of that elusive ideological transition to the mentalities of the slave trade and plantation slavery. It is reported, for example, that the first auction of African captives imported into Portugal in the 1440s 'was interrupted by the common folk, who were enraged at seeing the separation of families of slaves'.[6] All such attitudes were rapidly swept away, and every humanist reaction was engulfed in a rising tide of greed. On all this the records are unrelievedly grim. Of the Portuguese who were looting India, wrote in 1545 the Christian missionary who was to become St Francis Xavier, 'there is here a power which I may call irresistible, to thrust men into the abyss where, besides the seductions of gain and the easy chance of plunder, their appetites for gain will be sharpened by having tasted it'.

The New World, beginning with the Caribbean, already lay in the pain of that abyss by 1545, and there were men in Europe, peering over its edge into what they saw below, who were shocked into protest. Merchants in Portugal and Spain – and, afterwards, mer-chants elsewhere as well, above all in England and France – had now to deal with the pricks of an uneasy conscience at the consequences of their booming trade in chattel slaves. The polemics of the time are clear on that; but they are also clear that ideological balm was quickly found and applied. And in this process, in this 'transition', one may see how and where the bedevilments of racism now began.

*   *   *

The arguments used to justify the mass reduction of captured Africans to the sub-human status of chattel enslavement show a clear trajectory of moral degradation. These arguments began in the Most Catholic Kingdoms of Spain and Portugal as presenting a means of spreading Christianity, of giving the means of Salvation to pagans otherwise condemned, ineluctably, to the fires of Hell. It could not be long, of course, before this kind of evangelism was lost in the verbiage of hypocritical claptrap; and this claptrap was to echo down the years until it reached its deafening chorus in the writings of Liverpool and

Bristol merchants of the 1770s. But it was meagre stuff at the best, and almost from the start it was seen that something more was needed if the slave trade were not to be threatened by abolition.

These captives, it was therefore soon being said, were fitted for enslavement because they lacked the capacities to know and use freedom: they belonged in truth to an inferior sort of humanity; in short, they were 'primitives' whom it was practically a mercy to baptise and enslave. Even before the middle of the fifteenth century, the Portuguese royal chronicler, Zurara, was able to assure the court in Lisbon that West Africans then being imported were 'sinful, bestial, and, because of that, naturally servile'.[7] And with *this* application of the idea that 'distance widens deviation from the norm', there appeared and rapidly flourished all that farrago of disgusting nonsense that was to take shape as the ideology of racism, whether in high-minded academic 'explanations' or the yobbery of saloon-bar gossip.

No doubt this ideology of justification for doing to blacks what Christianity and law alike forbade Europeans to do to whites came in many ingenuities and subtleties of gloss. There is no need in these columns to enlarge upon them. The point here is that the ideology of this justification grew and developed in the measure that the overseas slave trade from Africa became enlarged from a trickle to a flood. After that, moreover, it was enlarged again when the overseas slave trade, in itself the product of a proto-colonial relationship between Europe and Africa, was transformed into the imperialism of the nineteenth century. Racism had been useful to the justification of mass enslavement. It was to be still more useful to the justification of invading and dispossessing Africans in their own lands, Africans at home, at a time when invading and dispossessing Europeans in their own lands, Europeans at home, was stridently deplored as an act of barbarism. Everyone knows this now, even if they seldom like to admit to knowing it, and there is again no need for me to insist upon the point. But I would like to look a little further into those crucial years when the 'racism' of superstition, of 'deviance', became transformed into the racism – without inverted commas – of hard cash.

*   *   *

When, in 1603, King James VI of Scotland and I of England followed Elizabeth to the throne of what was not yet Britain (insofar, that is, as 'Britain' has ever become a cultural reality), it could not be said that the English were a racist people. As it happened, they were not even a particularly superstitious people in the sense that superstition feeds racism: after the 1540s, the Reformation had increasingly seen to that. They were going to become a racist people in the fullest 'hard cash'

meaning of the term, but that was going to take some time to happen.
The case of *Othello*, surely one of Shakespeare's finest plays, is there
to suggest some of the complexities along this route of transition.
Written in 1603 or 1604, just when the Elizabethan age was passing
away, *Othello* was played to London audiences for whom the slave
trade in captives seized in Africa – to the extent that those audiences
could have been aware of the trade – was the work and monopoly of
England's mortal enemies of Spain and Portugal (the latter being then
part of the Spanish realm). It was not a trade in which English
venturers can have wished to have any but a marginal or purely
piratical part. But times were changing.

England would become expansionist, would carve out colonies in
the Caribbean, would embark upon the slave trade, would eventually
become the greatest slaving power of all. And for all this, the
necessary mental transitions were already under way. This is what we
see and hear in *Othello*. The play itself, as C.L.R. James used rightly
to insist, is in no substance a racist play, and to see it as such is to have
misunderstood the motives of the drama, motives concerned above all
with careerism, distrust of foreigners, and sexual jealousy: the 'classic'
motives, in short, of the Elizabethan theatre when dramatising the
frailties of humankind. Yet the motives of racism have already edged
their way into the scenario. Othello is the mighty general of the armies
of the Republic of Venice, and entrusted by the rulers of Venice with
the defence of their interests and empire in the Mediterranean Sea.
Even the traitorous Iago has to admit 'the Moor – howbeit that I
endure him not – is of a constant loving noble nature'. And when Iago
dies as a despised traitor, Othello meets – at least in the Elizabethan
view – a most honourable death. But the Moor's features and
physique are nonetheless made to serve Iago's purpose. Racism is on
the way and, in England, will begin to flourish within less than half a
century.

A.C. de C.M. Saunders is entirely right when he says in his most
useful book (to which I would like to draw attention here) that 'the
introduction of black slaves into Portugal marks a turning point in the
history of slavery'. It marks this turning point not because that
introduction, in itself, brought anything new to the scene. It does so
because it led directly, and within a handful of years, to the massive
export of captives from Africa for chattel enslavement in the Americas. And this was made possible, in turn, because Christopher
Columbus had 'discovered America'. That is why this 'history of
slavery' is, no less, the history of modern imperialism, for without the
slave trade, the 'conquests' across the Atlantic must soon have
withered for lack of the labour to exploit them. Without mass
enslavement, in short, there would have been no trans-Atlantic
European empires save for the initial looting and sacking of material

wealth. The track followed by the maturity of capitalism would have been a different one, and very conceivably a less ruthless and destructive one.

Anyone who cares to toil through the archives of the partition of Africa, and its consequences after 1900, when that partition was made more or less complete, will soon find reason to ponder on all this. For the partition of Africa and other such activities in the history of modern imperialism all lead back to the birth of an instrumentalist racism. The dead hand of Columbus, clutching in its icy grasp the 'certainties' of white superiority in one guise or another, and therefore the destinies of black subjection, is there to shake its ghastly warning as surely as did Banquo's ghost at Macbeth's triumphal feasting, and evoke Macbeth's response:

Avaunt, and quit my sight! Let the earth hide thee!
Thy bones are marrowless, thy blood is cold . . .

And yet, we know with what malignant power the bones and blood of this racism could operate. Calling up this Banquo's ghost at the festivities in celebration of Columbus may be tactless, even in poor taste. Yet I have the hope that some awareness of the curse that Columbus laboured to lay upon mankind may occur at this time, and induce – what shall I say – a certain sobriety, even a sense of shame.

References

1   S.D. Goitein, *A Mediterranean Society: Vol 1 Economic Foundations* (Los Angeles, 1967), pp 130-31.
2   A.C. de C.M. Saunders, *A Social History of Black Slaves and Freedmen in Portugal 1441-1555* (Cambridge, 1982), introduction and Ch.1 passim.
3   All this is made clear from an analysis of the relative costs of purchase and maintenance of slaves in medieval times, an aspect of 'labour history' that is much in need of detailed synthesis. We find, for instance, that in medieval Cairo, according to Goitein (op. cit.) working from contemporary documents, 'In and out of bondage, the slave was a member of the family' (p145), while 'the acquisition of a male slave was a great affair, on which a man was congratulated almost as if a son had been born to him. No wonder, for a slave fulfilled tasks similar to those of a son' (p132).
4   Herodotus, *The Histories*, in translation of Aubrey de Selincourt (Harmonds-worth, 1954), p247.
5   John Middleton, *Lugbara Religion* (Oxford, 1960), especially pp 230ff.
6   Saunders, op. cit., p35.
7   Ibid., p39, relying largely on Zurara's contemporary chronicle and other contemporary sources.

500 Years OF RESISTANCE CAMPAIGN

On July 10th 1991, in committee room 10 of the Houses of Parliament, the campaign **500 Years of Resistance** was launched by over 20 national organisations working with Latin America and the Caribbean.

The campaign is the national committee of an initiative in the Americas which has brought together the indigenous, black and popular movements of Latin America, North America and the Caribbean.

The campaign will work over the coming year to present the other side of the history and consequences of Columbus's invasion. Already, there are 16 local committees of the campaign in all areas of Britain and more are being formed.

The priority issues of the campaign will be:

★ Human Rights in the Americas
★ The North-South relationship
★ The External Debt
★ Environmental and Natural Resources
★ Refugees and Economic Migrants in Europe.

Join us and help to build a broad movement of opposition to the official celebrations of Columbus's voyage.

....

I/we would like to join the 500 Years of Resistance campaign and enclose
☐ £6 (individuals)   ☐ £4 (unwaged individuals)
☐ £15 (local organisations)   ☐ £50 (National organisations)

I/we enclose a donation of ....

Please return to: 500 Years of Resistance, Priory House, Kingsgate Place, London NW6 4TA

MICHAEL STEVENSON

Columbus and the war on indigenous peoples

In 1992 it will be 500 years since Columbus journeyed west across the Atlantic Ocean in search of personal fortune, spiritual destiny and the fabulous riches of the East. Cecil Jane observes that Columbus hoped 'he might acquire riches, fame and honour becoming a viceroy and governor-general, taking rank among the mightiest princes of the earth'.[1] Pauline Watts notes that there was a powerful millenarian strain in Columbus's aspirations. She quotes from a letter he wrote in 1500: 'God made me the messenger of the new heaven and the new earth of which he spoke in the Apocalypse of St John after having spoken of it through the mouth of Isaiah; and he showed me the spot where to find it.'[2]

Today, we can see that to one set of human beings this opening up of new worlds brought opportunities offered by spices, sugar, tobacco, coffee, cacao, gold, silver, forests and fertile lands. For the other set of humans, living rich and viable lives, the Columbian journey spelt disease, humiliation, destruction of culture and living conditions, and mass death.

It was with this 'encounter' – a neutral word, chosen by the victors – that a process of destruction, so all-encompassing and systematic that it can only be described as 'total war', was inaugurated by Europeans against indigenous peoples. The central endeavour was, and still is, to lay waste a people and destroy their culture in order to undermine the integrity of their existence and appropriate their riches. Powered by

Michael Stevenson lectures in anthropology and sociology at Monash University, Melbourne, Australia.

Race & Class, 33, 3 (1992)

predatory appetite, fuelled by culture and belief, total war (which, in this sense, entails not only the physical destruction of children, women, men, but the devastation of their material and spiritual economy) continually recreates its mechanisms of justification. In the process, it builds up a structure of collective feeling, a way of thought and a language that facilitates its continuity from generation to generation. What characterises total war is the comprehensiveness and viciousness of its assault which, to be sustained, demands that 'the enemy' be deemed not simply an opponent to be defeated, but as a thing to be eradicated.

As situations, technologies, methods change, so 'total war' has to be understood in its historical contexts. It emerged in the Old World and, by way of the colonising process, was carried to the New World, where it took root and expanded. In the nineteenth and twentieth centuries, total war combined with racism, nationalisms and imperialism to become globalised. But it is instructive of later developments to look back at the inception of the processes that were to wreak such havoc.

When Europeans moved out of their home territories, encountering new peoples and social worlds, they began to forge a complex of words and conduct which enabled them to define their own humanness, even as they appropriated the wealth and lives of indigenous peoples. And it is such phrases and concepts which became decisive components in the methodology of total war. To put it differently, in the making of the modern world a special language was developed, refined and, as time passed, consolidated by diverse groups which, in this process of discovery and exploration, formed a sense of themselves as the Spanish, the French, the English, the Portuguese, and as the Europeans. The use of this language and the inevitability of hierarchy that it conveyed underpinned an array of brutal techniques by which whole cultures were uprooted or destroyed in the drive for the expansion of production and exchange. Such language functioned to provide those groups using it with not only a rationale for action, but also a heroic and noble sense of identity as they went into the battle. The development of this special language also gave particular groups of Europeans an anchorage in an era in which they suffered from severe ontological anxieties unleashed by the upheavals associated with the transitions from feudalism to capitalism, and the sudden expansion of their universe. Thus, in a situation of complicated and traumatic power struggles at home, the language of total war fashioned in and for Europe provided the colonisers with the psychological momentum and confidence to determine the fates and the identities of masses of human beings. The words and phrases manifested an alchemic faith that much, if not all, was transmutable.

Legal issues and modes of perception

The meeting between the peoples of the Old and New Worlds, symbolised by Columbus's journey, was but the beginning of a dynamic movement out of Europe that eventually became global. It raised legal questions that could not be disentangled from ethical and political issues. Indeed, the matters arising from these relationships remain unresolved to this day and everywhere continue to be a source of labyrinthine and deadly conflicts. The colonising process entailed entering and destroying people's domains, and developing methods of disciplinary control over their lives, while devising various techniques for taking their lands. Those directing such processes required rules, embedded in an all-purpose language in order to give direction to their decisions while seeking legitimacy for their actions in the midst of turmoil. I am not concerned here with providing a history of international laws or national legal systems as they emerged out of the disintegration of western feudalism, but with illustrating the connection between the words and the legal issues, and noting some of the patterns.

David Bears Quinn, the doyen of transatlantic history, observes that, under Elizabeth I, an 'American' party emerged, led by men such as Sir Humphrey Gilbert, his half-brother Sir Walter Raleigh and diverse others, and that when James I ascended the throne in 1603, the pent-up colonising energies of the English were co-ordinated and unleashed upon north-east America.[3] These energies were focused and expressed in the formation of the Virginia Company. In the beginning, the English wanted to sell English cloth and metal objects to the Native Americans, believed that they could grow Mediterranean-type agricultural products in Virginia and hoped to find precious metals. Ordinary English men and women were willing to leave home, but they wanted land so that families could exploit small or moderate-sized holdings, and that meant trouble with the Amerindian peoples. 'What is clear', says Quinn, is that the Europeans 'believed they had a right to enter and occupy lands in any part of North America they fancied, without any regard for the rights and the safety, even the survival, of those whose rights had been ensured for millennia.' Olive Patricia Dickason points out that Christians could take Amerindian territories and force the inhabitants to accept baptism, as long as they were acting for their monarchs.[4] By classifying the Amerindian peoples as heathens (i.e., as 'savages'[5]), she argues, Europeans further reinforced the accepted view that Christians had the right to take control of the non-Christian New World. Leading international jurists of the day made the case. In 1532, Francisco de Vitoria (1486-1546), primary professor of sacred theology at the University of Salamanca and a Dominican, argued that although the

Aztecs and the Incas wore clothes and were politically organised in ways Europeans understood, their conquest was justified 'on the grounds of violations of natural law: human sacrifice and cannibalism[6] in the case of the Mexicans, tyranny and the deification of the Inca in the case of the Peruvians'. Albert Gentili (1552-1608), regius professor of civil law at the University of Oxford and Protestant by religion, argued that war was justifiable against Native Americans because they 'practiced abominable lewdness' and engaged in sins contrary to human nature. Hugo Grotius (1583-1645), jurist and diplomat, and also Protestant, moralised that the 'most just war is against savage beasts, the next against men who are like beasts'. Gentili defended the European seizure of unoccupied lands 'even though such lands belong to the sovereign of that territory', on the grounds 'of the law of nature which abhors a vacuum', and then remarked, 'is not almost all of the New World unoccupied?'

By 1514, the Spanish had invented a legal convention that would fend off criticism of their behaviour by other Europeans. A special proclamation (*requerimento*) would be read in Spanish to any concentrations of native people the invaders encountered, commanding them to become the subjects of Spain and accept Christianity. If they did not acquiesce (and how could they, asks Quinn), then they could be treated as enemies and enslaved.[7] Finally, Dr Juan Ginés de Sepúlveda, in his famous debate in 1550 with Dominican friar Bartolomé de las Casas, argued that the beings of the New World were only fit for conquest and enslavement. They 'lack culture', do not 'know how to write', 'keep no records of their history' and 'do not have written laws'; further, before the arrival of the Christian Spanish, they 'were involved in every kind of intemperance and wicked lust', made 'war continuously and ferociously against each other', and were addicted to satisfying 'their monstrous hunger with the flesh of their enemies', yet they were 'so cowardly and timid' that thousands of them flee 'like women before a very few Spaniards'.[8]

In these statements, all uttered within the first sixty years of Columbus's landfall, a new doctrine was being fashioned, albeit from the old notions about the 'other'. In them, there is a striving to invest the conception of the 'savage' with flesh-and-blood realism, and to bring to bear economic, political, legal, ethical and religious ideas on this representation. The lands of the 'savages' are deemed empty of civilisation and thus open to occupation and economic, political, legal, ethical and religious development; such beings cannot establish rational or viable political organisation and, therefore, are prone to inchoate and murderous strife; their religious impulses are heinous and corrupt. The term 'civilisation' begins to be vested with enlightenment meanings. The humanness of those who dwell in the New World is a deceit of the senses, is not real. Their erotic life is without order or moral discipline and so the evil animality of these beings is expressed in their insatiable appetite for each other's flesh. Amerigo Vespucci assured his readers that 'human flesh is a common article of diet with them . . . the father has already been seen to eat children and wife, and I knew a man . . . who was reputed to have eaten more than three hundred human bodies . . . I saw salted human flesh suspended from beams between the houses, just as with us it is the custom to hang bacon and pork' and, in the same breath, 'The women . . . are very libidinous . . . When they had the opportunity of copulating with Christians, urged by excessive lust, they defiled and prostituted themselves.'⁹ Here is a gender line of attack, coming as it does from persons infatuated with power. Fathers eat wives and children, men are effeminate – they run away like women – and women lack restraint or decorum, are dominated by lust and are incapable of loyalty. The lascivious, illiterate, cowardly yet ferocious cannibal, who is incapable of a genuine economic and legal life, begins to haunt European life. At its heart, the cannibal metaphor emphasises violent, unpredictable, demonic consumption.

The invention and application of such language, replete with its vivid imagery of the grotesque, provides its composers with advantages. The use of these words suppresses their human capacity to identify with the 'other'. The litanic repetition ensures an in-built, structured inhibition of the dangerous growth of feelings of empathy, compassion and the sense of a shared humanity. There are distinct economic and political gains in such enduring inhibition because the new class relations that develop among the Europeans themselves through the colonising process do, at times, take on a savage bitterness. Through a common adherence to a common mode of thought, expressed in a common language, the path to continued colonial expansion is not only eased, but also the fragmentation arising from mutually destructive strife is held in check. For the new ruling elite, such a process helps maintain its economic and political power, and puts it in the position of being able to offer prizes to the strata below. Only the peoples who are savages or barbarians need not be conceded the religious, political, legal and economic graces.

There are other gains in developing these phrases. Adopting such a psycho-linguistic position is advantageous to the group that covets the lands, the gold and the bodies of the others. An express characterisation masks predatory action and intention. Hence, the statements invariably combine passion with a tough-minded economic action. The intrepid Captain John Smith, a founding father of Virginia, in his *Map of Virginia* (1612) gives a meticulous description of a rich and bountiful land carefully cultivated by its original inhabitants and then declares that the English have found a place, 'a nurse for soldiers, a practise for mariners, a trade for marchants . . . and . . . a businesse (most acceptable to God) to bring such poore infidels to the true knowledge of God and his holy Gospell'.[10] He goes on to observe that the chief 'God they worship is the Divell', and 'They say they have conference with him, and fashion themselves as neare to his shape as they can imagine'. It was a common belief that Satan was active in the New World. Protestant minister Alexander Whitaker, in his *Good Newes from Virginia* (1613), records that although the Indians acknowledge a 'great good God', it is the devil who they truly fear and worship, and that the people are slaves to their priests who are the same as 'our English Witches'.[11] Whitaker also informed his country-men that the Indians 'esteem it a virtue to lie, deceive and steale as their master the divell teacheth to them.'[12] Wildness was a frequent theme in this economic and religious reasoning: the land 'is inhabited with wild and savage people, that live and lie up and downe in troups like heards of Deere in a Forrest', wrote another early Virginian.[13] The combination of economic aspiration joined with the religious impulse is nicely expressed in a statement issued by the Virginia Company in 1610 that spelt out the English offer to the Powhatans: we, 'by way of merchandizing and trade, doe buy of them the pearles of the earth and sell to them the pearles of heaven'.[14]

In 1622, the Powhatans rose against the English, rejecting both trade and the Christian God and His holy gospel. They chose to protect their lives and their lands as the English settled in and planted tobacco wherever they could. Captain John Smith expressed his fury, describing the Powhatans as a 'perfidious and inhumane people', 'cruel beasts' with 'a more natural brutishness than beasts'.[15] It was the one hundred and thirtieth year of the Columbian era, and the shift in human circumstance begun by his voyage had taken root in the Virginian soil. In the history of total war, this was the first decisive moment for the Europeans to harvest the fruit of the language planted in American soil. It spelt annihilation for the Native American peoples constituting the Powhatan confederacy.[16]

In the language, a link is forged between the devil and economic backwardness. To kill such beings, constituted as they are of incon-sistent negativities, is an expression of economic rationality, moral purpose and religious commitment. Yet the constant reiteration of these ideas points to a collective anxiety about intentions, a troubling about predatory conquest, about agonistic behaviour,[17] about giving uninhibited vent to the acquisitive passions. (We remember the turmoil of the Reformation and the grim struggles of the English Civil War.) Perhaps a battle is being fought out in the European imagin-ation and conscience and yet, at the same moment, there is an intense searching around for the appropriate transformative formulae so that potential energies can be unleashed without hindrance. Given this emphasis upon words and conception, it is no accident that, by 1596, only 100 years after Columbus's first voyage, an Elizabethan poet, gentleman and colonist was striving to articulate the correct method to transform the Irish and Ireland so that, in his eyes, a flourishing and progressive civilisation might be established. I refer to Edmund Spenser's *A View of the Present State of Ireland*.[18]

As time passed, and after considerable strife, the colonial settlers began to see themselves as a nation and the language to assume an august, elegiac quality, yet the economic element remained. On 28 May 1830, President Andrew Jackson signed the Indian Removal Act which gave the president authority to remove all those west of the Mississippi river. On 6 December 1830, he declared in his second annual message, 'Humanity has often wept over the fate of the aborigines of this country . . . one by one have many powerful tribes disappeared from the earth. To follow to the tomb the last of his race and to tread on the graves of extinct nations excite melancholy reflections . . . [but] what good man would prefer a country covered with forests and ranged by a few thousand savages to our extensive Republic'.[19] Although 200 years have passed since the founding of Virginia, the words still draw on the images of wildness, and reiterate the concept of terra nullis. Once again, the themes of death and development are linked in the European imagination ('just war against men who are like beasts', 'the law of nature which abhors a vacuum'). But, in 1830, North America was on the eve of a new capitalism, an industrial kind, and so the language becomes the basis for the forming of national identity and for providing the state with an organising ideology. The president's people have an inherent right and capacity to expand, to transform nature. The impotence of extinction is the alternative. The legal domain is no longer that of theological jurists of Christendom; it has become institutionalised as the democratic nation-state which develops laws in its assemblies, laws upheld by an international, that is, imperialist morality.

The same language that was fashioned by the dictates of the colonists was also what informed and shaped their laws. On 8 February 1887, the General Allotment Act became federal law in the United States. It authorised the president to divide an 'Indian' reservation into individual holdings, assign a parcel of land to each man, woman and child, and to declare all remaining land surplus to the needs of the 'Indians'. The 'surplus' lands were opened up for homesteading, with each acre costing the settlers $2.50. Between 1887 and 1930, Native Americans lost two-thirds of their severely diminished land base, that is, 90 million acres.[20] Senator Pendleton of Ohio supported the legislation in congress with these words:

They must either change their mode of life or they must die . . .
these Indians must either change . . . or they will be exterminated
. . . We must stimulate within them . . . the idea of home, of
family, and of property. These are the very anchorages of civilisation; the commencement of the dawning of these ideas in the mind
is the commencement of the civilisation of any race and these
Indians are no exception.[21]

The feudal era has passed and it is 400 years since Columbus's first
journey, yet the words still speak of the extermination of Indian
culture; now, however, the language also bespeaks settled bourgeois
values. Private property, order and life lie on one side, 'Indianness',
disorder and death on the other. The structured inhibition of identifi-
cation with the Indian remains, and so the language continues to do its
work. The vituperative vision expressed by Captain John Smith after
the Powhatan attack devastated the first colony is echoed in Senator
Pendleton's words, but the hostility is now structured into the
developed legal codes of the nation state. The hatred is bureaucrat-
ised.

The 'savage' and underdevelopment

But there is a paradox embedded in the language. There is constant
repetition of the image of empty landscapes dotted with a few 'herds'
of 'savages'. The savage is incapable of regeneration, is few in
numbers, is weak, lacks vigour, and is incapable of cultivating the soil.
Yet these same savages treacherously mass in numbers, manifest
demonic ferocity, and overwhelm the civilised European. The Reverend Samuel Purchase, writing in the 1620s, describes the Powhatans
of Virginia. At first he is generous. In so far as the Indians live
according to the law of nature, the European cannot expect them to
work the 'land according to God's revealed will. Still, the English, as
Christians knowing God's will, have an obligation to work that land;
for it is almost bare of inhabitants' and is rich in those things 'which
make for merchandise'.[22] But once the Indians rise against the
English, legal restraints arising from the laws of nature can be put
aside and, directed by their God, the English have the right to do as
they please, 'God is to be glorified as this rich and abundant Virginia is
properly used'. The deracinating functions of the language emerge.
The savage inhabitants have 'little of Humanitie but shape, ignorant
of Civilitie, of Arts, of Religion; more brutish than the beasts they
hunt, more wild and unmanly than that unmanned wild Countrey,
which they range rather than inhabite'. Purchase goes on to observe
that the Powhatans are in the grip of Satan and, being devoted to his
cause, indulge in 'mad impieties' and 'wicked idleness'. No doubt the

literate ideologists of colonialism, such as Purchase, drew on the phrases of the ancients in developing the appropriate language. Odysseus narrates: 'And we came to the land of the Cyclopes, a fierce, uncivilised people who never lift a hand to plant or plough . . . All the crops they require spring up unsown and untilled . . . The Cyclopes have no assemblies for the making of laws . . . live in hollow caverns in the mountain heights, where each man is lawgiver to his children and his wives.'

In English Virginia, the savages are few in numbers and are in the grip of degenerative lusts and satanic idleness, whereas the proper Christian behaviour is economic. The insurmountable drawback of the Indians is that they cannot produce wealth in its appropriate form. The Virginian savages are incapable of forming laws, and so have no legal relation to the land. They merely range as wild beasts do. It follows that those Englishmen who leave the colonial settlement choosing to live with them are retrieved, tortured and even put to death.[23] It also follows that, given the savages' inherent tendencies, it becomes a religious duty to put them to the sword if they hinder God's spiritual and economic aspirations being realised; total war becomes an act of religious purification that rids the landscape of satanic forces. Reverend Purchase is thus a tribal priest who draws boundaries, and the effect of his language is to tribalise the situation, thereby overcoming Christianity's ecumenical tendency. The words, by focusing feelings of difference, facilitate the building of a powerful sense of identity enabling personal and collective energies to be unleashed.

Colonising situations are dangerous because the internal rivalries and animosities of the colonists, added to the stresses of the pioneering situation, may lead them to turn on each other. Thus, projecting malevolent forces outside the colonial tribe contributes to solidarity and assists cooperation, particularly once power struggles break out amongst the settlers.[24] The point is that early settlers have meagre material resources such as seeds, few instruments and limited life supporting goods (food, fuel, clothing and so on). Therefore, they must rely on cultural goods, such as skills, and ideas that provide conceptions of moral order and the good life. Such ideas enable the settlers to convert the strange and new nature they have found into familiar culture. They strive to control and dominate nature. As the colonists appropriate land, they exclude the indigenous people, unless they can be subordinated and put to use in creating the good life. The economics of scarcity is a concept which excludes at an ideological level all the Indians, although, practically, only those who the settlers come across are exterminated. Finally, the colonists suspend ecumenical values to the point that prevents the passive participants in genocide from passing judgement upon the active ones.

Much is made of the lack of numbers of the indigenous people.

Whereas earlier it stood for terra nullis, later on it stands for weakness, failure, political, military and economic impotence. The juxtaposition with reality is intriguing. Henry Dobyns argues that Native American peoples living north of Mesoamerica numbered about eighteen million, and that they practised an economic life that made such numbers possible and viable.[25] But, from 1520, the presence of the Spanish, Portuguese, French, Dutch and English spread wave upon wave of catastrophic epidemics of diseases (chickenpox, influenza, typhus, whooping cough, malaria, dengue (breakbone fever), yellow fever, and syphilis – the evidence that European sailors contracted syphilis from women in the Caribbean islands is no longer persuasive. These realities gave epistemological veracity to the European's savage. Frances Jennings points out that because scholars regarded New World cultures as being savage, they believed that large populations were inconceivable. She criticises and refutes the arguments of two American anthropologists, James M. Mooney and Louis Kroeber, observing that both men contended that, before Columbus, North America, excluding Mexico, supported only one million humans.[26] Kroeber's ratio of man to land for the total area of Canada and the United States amounts to one person per seven square miles. Kroeber rejected the idea that Native Americans were capable of 'ordering their societies and technologies so as to increase their populations beyond a static and sparsely distributed token representation'. Further, he reasoned that Indian societies were characterised by 'insane, unending, continuously attritional warfare and by the absence of all effective political organisation, and of the idea of the state'. Finally, although he knew that many agriculturally-based societies existed in north-east America, he discounted their capacity to produce surpluses, arguing that they were 'agricultural hunters' who refused to develop their land, much of which remained 'virgin', being regarded as 'hunting ground', and as 'waste'. In all this, holds Jennings, Kroeber was faithfully reproducing an enduring ideological tradition. Jennings then turns to research which reveals that, within a century of the Spanish invasion, the Native American population of Mexico shrank from about twenty-five million to under two million, that is, a decline of 90 per cent. About the mode of demise she writes: 'Not even the most brutally depraved of the conquistadors was able purposely to slaughter Indians on the scale that the gentle priest unwittingly accomplished by going from his sickbed ministrations to lay his hands in blessing on his Indian converts.'[27]

The Caribs, the Irish, the Powhatans and the Pequots

European diseases were not the only exterminators of the millions of humans living in the Caribbean, Mexico and northern America. In his journey into the New World, Columbus claimed he discovered two kinds of beings. One lot, he wrote, were not 'fitted' to use weapons, were 'marvellously timorous', 'guileless', 'content with whatever trifle of whatever kind that may be given them', yet 'they should be good servants' because 'they would easily be made Christians' and were of 'quick intelligence', and 'very soon say all that is said to them'. Thus, 'when your Highnesses so command, they can all be carried off to Castile or held captive in the island itself' to be 'kept in subjection and forced to do whatever may be wished'.[28] These were labelled the Arawaks. The other beings were 'fierce', 'eat human flesh' and 'have many canoes with which they range through all the islands . . . and pillage and take . . . and are ferocious among these other people who are cowardly to an excessive degree'. Columbus labelled this second group Caribs, and recommended to the Spanish monarchs that they be sold into slavery. At the time that Columbus formed these categories, neither he, nor any of his entourage, could speak the indigenous languages.

Richard Moore asserts that the use of the word 'cannibal', with its 'false and vicious notions' begins with Columbus and that this accusation of 'common and widespread cannibalism' on the part of the Carib people debases them and, even to this day, 'defiles their name and defames their memory'. Moore suggests the manner in which Columbus fabricated the image of the Caribs as ferocious man-eaters, and delineates his role in branding them as fierce anthropophagi. Columbus was well acquainted with the slave trade because, before he journeyed to the New World, he had travelled 'to Guinea on the West Coast of Africa and knew of the slave marts of Portugal and Spain'. And he sought crafty justifications by declaring that the indigenous people he met used Carib and kindred names to refer to the terrifying enemies they feared. 'Under the influence of the medieval mythology and travel accounts he had read in *The Book of Marco Polo* and *Mandeville's Travels* Columbus' rendered 'such indigenous terms as *caritaba, cariba* and *caribal* as *canima, caniba* and *canibal*'.[29] Thus, Columbus designed the notion that the Carib were compulsive anthropophagi by connecting Carib, the name of the people, to cannibal, meaning monstrous man-eater. He made up this representation, Moore contends, so that he could recommend to the Spanish monarchs a trade in slaves. He urged the King and Queen repeatedly to sanction Carib slavery and, in 1503, overcoming their religious qualms, they authorised the settlers to enslave the Caribbean peoples because, as they wrote in their proclamation, such beings 'are hardened in their bad habits of idolatry and cannibalism', thus sounding the death-knell for millions in the Caribbean area.

Nancie Gonzalez adds further precision to Richard Moore's account. She notes that it was the Taino whom Columbus first met,

because at that time they 'inhabited the Greater Antilles, the
Bahamas, and other northernmost islands of the Caribbean'.[30] They
belonged to the Arawakan language and culture group, and were
decimated by disease, colonial warfare, and enslavement. In the
Lesser Antilles there lived another socio-cultural group, also Arawakan, but now known as Caribs. They had called themselves Kalipuna
or Callinago, depending on whether the speaker was male or female.
Europeans portrayed them as being extremely warlike because they
defended themselves against the colonial settlers effectively, and so
were depicted as 'aggressive, vicious, ruthless, well-organised and
suitable only for extermination or enslavement'. The royal decree of
1503 invested the term 'Carib' with a special meaning: it became the
'official designation for hostile Indians subject to capture and sale'.[31]
The Spanish conquistador, Juan de Castellos, in fact admitted this
distorted meaning: 'they were called Caribs not because they would
eat human flesh but because they defended their homes well'.
Ironically, in the indigenous language, Carib means 'brave, daring', or
'extraordinary man, valiant man'.[32]

The word cannibal was thus invested with a number of meanings. It
referred to any group of indigenous people who mounted effective
resistance to the European coloniser, who were to be exterminated
and whose riches the coloniser wished to appropriate. Yet, essentially,
the world cannibal expresses the colonisers' desire to consume human
bodily power in the form of forced labour. The labourer is the beast to
be worked unto death.

There is an irony here. Edmund Morgan records that, in the early
years of Virginia, the English found it difficult to organise an effective
agrarian economy. This resulted from their internal social difficulties.
On the other hand, the Powhatans not only grew corn but occasionally
traded it with the settlers. For the Powhatans, the country was also
rich in game, geese and ducks. For the English, who lacked the skills
of hunting and knowledge of ways of the animals, and who also held
an aversion to hunting for food, the country was bare, untamed.* So,
by the winter of 1609-10, after three planting seasons had passed, the
500 settlers were starving and, in fact, presented 'the only authentic
examples of cannibalism in Virginia'. One provident man chopped up
his wife and salted down the pieces. Others dug up graves to eat the
corpses. By spring, only sixty were left alive.[33]

Two historians, Nicholas Patrick Canny and Frances Jennings,
demonstrate the connections between colonisation and the methods
of total war. Canny's thesis is that Englishmen transferred to Virginia
and New England a method of war which they had developed and

---

* In English culture hunting was practised by the upper classes for pleasure. Poaching
was done by the poor and the destitute; it was thieving.

refined in Ireland in the sixteenth and seventeenth centuries.[34] Canny asserts that no historian 'has dealt with the legal and ethical considerations raised by colonisation in Ireland or with the means by which these were resolved to the satisfaction of the aggressors' consciences'. He shows 'how the justifications for colonisation influenced or reflected English attitudes towards the Gaelic Irish, and, by extension, towards the imported slave and the indigenous populations in North America'. Canny goes on to argue that 'sixteenth century Englishmen who pondered the Irish problem did so in secular terms, and . . . through their thinking on the social condition of the Irish, they approached a concept of cultural evolution'.

In 1559, the year after Elizabeth I succeeded to the throne, she changed England's official religion to Church of England, and, six years later in 1565, it became the avowed policy of her government to bring all of Ireland under English control. The key Elizabethan colonial adventurers in Ireland were members of the English gentry and the cadets of aristocracy. Each coloniser was privately sponsored and thus each had to justify aggression anew for himself.

The first step, writes Canny, was to be 'absolved from all normal ethical restraints', in other words, to feel free to assert that 'the natives were outside the law of moral obligation'.[35] The English colonisers in Ireland were able to do so by developing a particular language. The Irish, that is the Gaelic Irish, were defined as being 'unreliable', not open to persuasion, and so could only 'be subdued by force'; they 'breach their faiths' and had shown a tendency to revolt. So, being a 'wicked race' they constituted a legitimate 'sacryfice to God'. They were 'pagan'. Thus, they 'have neither feare nor love of God in their harts' and they 'blaspheme, they murder, commit whoredome' and all kinds of 'abomination without scruple of conscience'. Being pagan also meant that the Irish were culturally backward barbarians. They were likened, therefore, to Huns, Vandals, Goths and Turks and described as 'little better than Cannibals who do hunt one another'.[36] They roamed about and did not make proper use of their land, were exceedingly licentious and prone to incest. In short, the colonising English defined the Irish as a lower order of humanity who 'live like beastes, voide of law and all good order' and who are most 'brutish in their customs'. This generation of colonisers replaced the old view of the Irish as socially inferior to the English with the novel idea 'that they were culturally inferior and far behind the English on the ladder of development'.[37] Such assertions gave licence to the systematic devastation of the Irish, which, besides other things, included the routine burning of crops and villages, the regular killing of women and children and the cutting off of heads, as well as the willingness to pay bounties for them – it brought 'great terrour to the people when thei sawe the hieddes of their dedde fathers, brothers, children, kinsfolke, and friendes'.[38] The theory and practice of total war involved premeditated terrorism.

Canny explores this issue with precision. He tells us that the colonising Elizabethan Englishmen justified their premeditation in these ways. It was strategically desirable to drive the Irish from the plains into the woods where they would freeze or famish with the onset of winter. This was justifiable because they were 'so wicked a race'. One master of terrorism was Sir Humphrey Gilbert who killed 'manne, woman and childe' so that 'the name of an Inglysh man was made more terryble'. For him, the slaughter of non-combatants was done to deprive the rebels of their support: 'so that the killyng of theim [women and children] by the sworde was the waie to kill the menne of warre by famine'. Sir Humphrey ordered that the heads of those killed in battle be cut off and laid in a laneway which led to his tent. The rationale was that 'through the terrour which the people conceived thereby it made short warres'.[39] The Norman lords had not committed such atrocities in Ireland, nor was systematic execution of non-combatants by martial law practised in any of the Tudor rebellions in England. In short, the English officers – most of whom were gentry – 'believed that in dealing with the native Irish population they were absolved from all normal ethical constraints'.[40] Jennings observes that the practice of burning villages and crops was transferred to America, especially when Native American guerrilla tactics prevented English victory. However, since 'according to Indian logic such destruction doomed non-combatants as well as warriors to die of famine during a winter without provisions', such extreme devastation was in their eyes irrational and broke their codes of war.[41]

In sum the English transferred to America four key usages discovered in Ireland:

> (1) a deliberate policy of inciting competition between natives in order, by division, to maintain control; (2) a disregard for pledges and promises to natives, no matter how solemnly made; (3) the introduction of total exterminatory war against some communities of natives in order to terrorise others; and (4) a highly developed propaganda of falsification to justify all acts and policies of the conquerors whatsoever. The net effect of all these policies in America has been the myth of the Indian Menace – the depiction of the Indian as a ferocious wild creature, possessed of an alternately demonic and bestial nature, that had to be exterminated to make humanity safe.[42]

On 26 May 1637, in a power struggle, a Puritan force massacred over 300 Pequot men, women and children at Mystic River, New England. Jennings comments: 'No Indian people has suffered more from this myth, either in its own time or in the historical records, than the

Pequots'.[43]

The Pequots have remained the subject of debate. Alfred Cave records that the Puritan historian William Hubbard, writing in 1677, asserted that the Pequots were not indigenous to southern New England and that they were 'a more fierce, cruel and warlike people than the rest of the Indians'.[44] Indeed, Hubbard went so far as to claim that shortly before the Pilgrims landed at Plymouth, Pequots had invaded coastal Connecticut from 'the interior of the continent' and, driving away the original inhabitants, 'by Force seized upon one of the goodliest places near the sea, and became a Terrour to all their Neighbours'. This representation of the Pequots as vicious, cruel and treacherous invaders to New England has been uncritically perpetuated throughout the historical record. After examining the various forms of evidence Cave concludes that:

> the Pequot invasion story was a belated embellishment to the Puritan propaganda of the Pequot War. The absence of corroborating testimony in contemporary documents written by Europeans raises doubts; archaeological and linguistic data suggest those doubts are well founded; and the depositions of seventeenth century Pequots and Narragansetts settle the issue.[45]

There was no Pequot invasion of New England. At best, William Hubbard misunderstood his informants, at the worst he spun a tale 'to give added force to his demonic characterisation of the Pequots'.[46] Remarkably, Cave is puzzled by the persistence of this tall story.

From 1622, under the leadership of Opechancanough, the Powhatans fought the English colonists in a struggle to ensure their survival. But, in 1646, the 80-year-old Powhatan leader was captured, 'placed on public exhibition like a caged animal', and then 'treacherously shot in the back by an English guard'.[47]

Conclusion

When Europeans made the Columbian journey, they reinforced a sense of themselves. By contraposition, they found the savage in order to reify their own diverse nationalisms, such as Spanish, Portuguese, Dutch, French and English. The archetypal event of colonisation, which is called discovery, continues to shape current realities in that the complex of words and conduct developed centuries ago still structures European modes of perceiving and organising. Even today, Australian Koories who lived in nineteenth-century 'Victoria' are described as ferocious cannibals. So are Mohawks in their fight for their land in Canada.

As the Old and the New Worlds joined, the various peoples of Europe generated a common rhetoric of conquest that gave them the momentum and the confidence to transform the identities, energies and living conditions of other human beings. The turning point occurred in an era in which Europeans of all classes suffered from severe anxieties aroused by the upheavals associated with the disintegration of the feudal world. Out of the traumatic experiences of this era, the persona of the 'savage' filled with contradictions was born. For the Europeans, the language of total war created a positive identity which fused humanness with trade, private property, capital accumulation through trade and investment, and progressive development. The counter identity created the other who was wild, inchoate and malevolent, able only to produce degenerative backwardness. An additional gain is that the words assisted the colonisers to forsake mutuality and to feel honourable as they subdued, disinherited and even exterminated the other.

Class systems build up hostile feelings in the groups which are compelled to order their lives and shape their needs according to such structures. When the forms of class systems undergo decisive and radical change, such feelings become volcanic. In the construction of the new class order, it assists the subject classes striving to establish themselves if the hatreds can be projected outwards. This was the case in Europe when the feudal world crumbled and the bourgeois world emerged. Therefore, the colonisers did not discover the degenerate barbarian and the cannibalistic savage; rather, they constructed such beings out of their own religious belief system. As Christians, the Europeans had from the very outset believed in dualisms of God and Satan, angels and devils, goblins and witches, wild men and wild women, but, most of all, absolute good and unmitigated evil. Before Columbus, there were no savage cannibals dwelling in the New World, but only hosts of peoples with their own identities, leading their own diverse modes of existence in their domains. The Europeans decided to call the place by a single name, America, and, once there, driven by material desire for wealth and power, blinded by self-justifying, religious belief, transformed the peoples into savages, some of them evil cannibals, others cowardly sub-humans; through their use of the methods of total war, the colonisers generated and sustained a new system of unequal relations which is still flourishing.

The European became an alchemist believing that he possessed special capacities and rights to transmute all that he touched. The Virginia Company, which represented a coalition of merchants and gentry devoted to the expansion of wealth and Christianity,[48] in 1609 instructed the governor of the colony, Sir Thomas Gates, that his missionaries should work with Indian children, and that he organise for them to be taken from their parents, since they were 'so wrapped up in the fogge and miserie of their iniquity and so tirrified with their continuall tirrany chayned under the bond of Deathe unto the Divell', that they would have to be forced into the Christian life.[49] The integrity of the indigenous identity and domain stood in the path of the European's ambition to transform the world after his own heart and so, driven on by unbridled arrogance, he compulsively sought to obliterate the identity of the indigene as a culturally rich and distinctive human being. The Virginia Company was a rapacious organisation and we can only conclude that its Christianity was not a sincere intention to bring enlightenment, but in fact was just one more weapon in the armoury aimed to transform those the European conquered into servants and slaves, chained to his alchemic enterprise.

References

1   See Cecil Jane (ed.), *The Four Voyages of Columbus* (New York, 1988); Pauline Moffit Watts, 'Prophecy and Discovery: on the spiritual origins of Christopher Columbus's "Enterprise of the Indies"', *American Historical Review* (Vol. 90, no. 1, 1985), pp. 73-102. See also Jan Carew, 'Columbus and the Origins of Racism in the Americas', *Race and Class* (Vol. XXIX, no. 4, 1988; Vol. 30, no. 1 1988).

2   P.M. Watts, 'Prophecy and discovery: on the spiritual origins of Christopher Columbus's "enterprise of the Indies"', *American Historical Review* (Vol. 90, no1, 1985), pp. 73-102.

3   D.B. Quinn, 'Colonies in the beginning: examples from North America' in Stanley H. Palmer and Dennis Reinhartz (eds), *Essays on the History of North American Discovery and Exploration* (Arlington, Texas, 1988).

4   O.P. Dickason, 'Old World Law: New World peoples, concepts of sovereignty' in Palmer and Reinhartz, op. cit.

5   The term 'savage' now carries serious complications for us. This is nicely argued by Claude Levi-Strauss in 'The future of anthropology' in his *Anthropology and Myth: lectures 1951-1982* (Oxford, 1987). He asks, 'Is anthropology condemned to become a science without an object?', and then observes, 'That object has traditionally been provided by the so-called 'primitive' peoples'. Amongst other difficulties, he draws attention to the conflict behind the formerly colonised peoples' opposition to anthropology. 'Their fear is that , beneath the semblance of a global ethnography, we seek to portray as a desirable *diversity* what appears to them as an intolerable *inequality*. With the best will in the world, we are not going to be accepted as their "savages". For, from the moment that we made them play this role, they ceased to exist for us; whereas, responsible in their eyes for their fate, we do exist for them'.

6   For the ritual and symbolic meanings of anthropophagy among the Amerindians and others, see inter alia, Claude Levi-Strauss, 'Cannibalism and ritual trans-vestism' op. cit., pp. 111-117. The main contention here is not whether there was cannibalism or not among the Indians, although it seems that the Caribs did not practise it. My concern is with the political meaning with which the settlers invested the practice and the practical uses to which they put the meaning. Further, it should be clear that the Europeans had fashioned the concept of cannibalism as a political one well before they left their native shores.

7   Quinn, op. cit.

8   In Robert F. Berkhofer, *The White Man's Indian* (New York, 1979), pp. 11-12, quoted from Lewis Hanke, *All Mankind is One* (De Kalb, Northern Illinois, 1974), p. 85. In an earlier work, Hanke illustrates the crafty manner in which de

Sepúlveda borrowed Aristotle's arguments justifying natural slavery in order to legitimise the Spanish settlers' killing and enslaving of the Amerindians. See Lewis Hanke, *Aristotle and the American Indians* (London, 1959).

9   R.F. Berkhofer, *The White Man's Indian* (New York, 1979), pp. 8-9

10   Philip L. Barbour (ed.), *The Complete Works of Captain John Smith, 1580-1631* (Chapel Hill, 1986).

11   Roy Harvey Pearce, *Savagism and Civilization: a study of the Indian and the American mind* (Berkeley, 1988), pp. 13-14.

12   Berkhofer, op. cit., p. 19.

13   Pearce, op. cit., p. 12.

14   Berkhofer, op. cit., pp. 117-8.

15   Frances Jennings, *The Invasion of America: Indians, colonialism, and the cant of conquest* (New York, 1976).

16   See J. Frederick Fausz, 'Opechancanough: Indian resistance leader' in David Sweet and Gary Nash (eds), *Struggle and Survival in Colonial America* (Berkeley, 1981); 'Patterns of Anglo-Indian aggression and accommodation along the mid-Atlantic coast, 1584-1634' in William W. Fitzhugh (ed.), *Cultures in Contact: the impact of European contacts on Native American cultural institutions AD 1000-1800* (Washington, 1985). See also E. Randolph Turner, 'Socio-political organisation within the Powhatan chiefdom and the effects of European contact AD 1607-1646' in Fitzhugh, op. cit.

17   I use the phrase in the ethological sense.

18   Edmund Spenser, *A View of the Present State of Ireland* edited by W.L. Renwick (Oxford, 1970). See also Nicholas Canny, 'Edmund Spenser and the development of an Anglo-Irish identity, in *The Yearbook of English Studies* (Vol. 13, 1983) and Nicholas Canny and Ciaran Brady, 'Debate: Spenser's Irish crisis: humanism and experience in the 1590s' in *Past and Present* (No. 120, 1988).

19   Pearce, op. cit., p. 57.

20   D'Arcy McNickle, 'Indian and European: Indian-White relations from Discovery to 1887' in *The Annals of the American Academy of Political Sciences* (Vol. 311, 1957).

21   Ibid.

22   Pearce, op. cit., pp. 7-8.

23   Edmund Morgan, *American Slavery American Freedom: the ordeal of colonial Virginia* (New York, 1975).

24   Carl Bridenbaugh, *Jamestown 1544-1699* (New York, 1980). He notes that, between December 1606 and February 1624, out of 7,289 colonists, 6,040 died. The dead were interred without ceremony or coffins lest the natives discover the truth. In 1616, 2,500 pounds of tobacco were shipped to England; and in 1628, 552,871. See also Barbour, op. cit., Jennings, op cit., p. 79 n66, and Morgan, op. cit.

25   Henry F. Dobyns, *Their Numbers Become Thinned: Native American population dynamics in eastern North America* (Knoxville, 1983). See also Neal Salisbury, *Manitou and Providence: Indians, Europeans and the making of New England, 1500-1643* (New York, 1982.)

26   Jennings, op. cit., pp.16-21

27   Ibid.

28   Richard B. Moore, *Caribs, 'Cannibals' and Human Relations* (New York, 1972) and Berkhofer, op. cit.

29   Moore, op. cit.

30   Nancie L. Gonzalez, 'From Cannibals to Mercenaries: Carib militarism, 1600-1840', *Journal of Anthropological Research* (Vol. 46, no. 1, 1990).

31   Ibid.

32   Moore, op. cit.

33 Morgan, op. cit., pp. 72-73ff. See also Jennings, op. cit., p. 79.
34 Nicholas P. Canny, 'The Ideology of English Colonisation: from Ireland to America', *The William & Mary Quarterly* (Vol. XXX, no. 4, 1973). Canny makes the following observation: 'David B. Quinn has stressed the connection between English colonisation in Ireland and the New World, and he has established the guidelines for a full investigation'.
35 Ibid. See also Jennings, op. cit., p. 212.
36 Canny, op. cit.
37 Ibid.
38 Ibid. See also Jennings, op. cit.
39 Canny, op. cit. In 1945, the same rationale was invoked to drop the atom bombs on Hiroshima and Nagasaki. In a suitable preamble, the Japanese too had been portrayed as less than human in the war and pre-war propaganda.
40 Ibid.
41 Jennings, op. cit.
42 Ibid.
43 Ibid.
44 Alfred A. Cave, 'The Pequot invasion of southern New England: a reassessment of the evidence', *The New England Quarterly* (Vol. LXII, no. 1, 1989); see also N. Salisbury, op. cit., for a full account of the Puritan destruction of the Pequots.
45 Cave, op. cit.
46 Ibid.
47 J.F. Fausz, op. cit., pp. 31-35
48 See Theodore K. Rabb, *Enterprise and Empire: merchant and gentry investment in the expansion of England 1575-1630* (Cambridge, Mass., 1967), pp. 2-4, 12-15, 19-38ff; also Quinn, op. cit, pp. 10-12 28-31.
49 See Pearce, op. cit., and Morgan, op. cit.

The myth

NANCY MURRAY

Columbus and the USA: from mythology to ideology

On Valentine's Day 1992, Barcelona's Christopher Columbus will marry the Statue of Liberty. The bride will be represented by a 100-foot long wedding cape, created by the Spanish artist, Miralda, who has been working on wedding plans for a decade. For months, the cape was displayed in New York's World Financial Center, so Lady Liberty could gaze at it from over the harbour. She could also theoretically gaze at a video-tape of her husband-to-be, playing on the widescreen television, which doubles as a gemstone on her engagement ring. The wedding cake, five storeys high, will be topped by a globe and the Eiffel Tower. Touted as a multinational affair drawing together artists and crafts-people from the US, Europe and Japan, and funding from such diverse sources as Pennsylvania Council on the Arts and Birmingham City Council in Britain, the ceremony will be consummated beneath the neon lights of Las Vegas.

The Columbus myth

Miralda's extravaganza is 'absolutely not' endorsed by the official US Christopher Columbus quincentenary jubilee convention, which was established by Congress during the Reagan years.[1] Perhaps his fusion of the 'discovery' of the New World and liberty in the cathedral of US culture was not reverent enough for the government officials and real estate magnates who dominate the commission's membership.

For the 'Columbus' whom the commission would have Americans

Nancy Murray is director of education for the Civil Liberties Union of Massachusetts.

Race & Class, 33, 3 (1992)

discover – or rather reaffirm * – is the Columbus around whom have crystallised the potent and self-celebratory myths which make up the national image and from which derive the 'American dream'. Columbus ('that first great entrepreneur' in the words of the commission's head) is the quintessence of the individual pioneer rolling back the frontier, of conquering and dynamic enterprise. It was Columbus whose actions broke through the dead weight of the old European feudal order and established a new from which could flow democracy, liberty, progress. It was Columbus who brought European values and culture to the new land, stamped it indelibly, in Schlesinger's phrase, as 'an off-shoot of Europe'.[2] For Columbus is celebrated, too, as the first European immigrant: the first of the Italians, Irish, Germans, Slavs, etc., who made up America, and from the many created the one: *e pluribus unum*.

It is this version of America that underlies the 200 or so national and international projects which bear the Commonwealth's logo – the memorabilia, the numerous statues of Columbus 'taking possession', the musical offerings with names like 'Rise, and sing America! – you owe it to Columbus', the formal civic ceremonies and garden shows in the plethora of towns named Columbus, the horseback ride across the country, the Order of the Sons of Italy torch relay, or the exhibit in Miami called the 'Cult of nature in Italian design'.

There are also the renamings, the parades, the films, TV shows and cultural events, featuring native arts and ethnic (Italian) displays. ** For the academically inclined, there are scholarships to study 'international economic development' and numerous symposia (including one called 'The perseverance of the indigenous peoples in the Americas', sponsored by 'Americans for Indian opportunity'). Finally, there are more ambitious projects – such as a yachting regatta across the Atlantic and the dispatching of spaceships to the 'new frontier', Mars.

But already the commission's project is coming unstuck, from contradictions within and opposition without. It has abandoned its sponsorship of a tour of Spanish-built replicas of the *Niña, Pinta* and *Santa Maria*. The commission's head, John Goudie, a Cuban immigrant turned Miami real estate speculator and Republican fundraiser, has been forced to resign under charges of corruption and nepotism. The 'public-private partnership' which offered, in the words of the commission's magazine, 'a unique opportunity for the private sector

---

* 'In 1492 Columbus discovered America. In 1992 America discovers Columbus', runs the official slogan.
** Federal support was withdrawn from a TV series which commission member Lynne Cheney, head of the National Endowment for the Humanities and spouse of the secretary of defence, claimed minimised the 'distressing aspects' of Aztec culture and maximised the 'excess' of the Spanish.

to band together in support of a cause which is non-controversial and universally appealing', has turned out to be something of a swindle, a microcosm of the larger economic order. And President Bush's call to individuals and corporations to give tax-deductible donations to enable the commission to commemorate, in a manner 'worthy of the boldness of Columbus and his crew', the 'New World's contribution to the Old World, particularly the common striving for freedom, democracy, and justice which binds us to the other nations in our hemisphere'[3], has had few takers. Investors are holding back, reluctant to sponsor projects which immediately become the targets of the 'alternative Columbus' protest movement, a rapidly burgeoning web of individuals, groups and coalitions which is determined to make 1992 a 'teachable moment', of economic and political reality and a celebration of 500 years of resistance.

The Native American groups forming 'alternative 1992' alliances, the church organisations like Clergy and Laity Concerned and the National Council of Churches and a variety of other groups, including various networks of educators, the Alliance for Cultural Democracy and the National Congress on Latin America (NACLA), which are putting together conferences, resources and curricula, the thousands of individuals around the country who are planning Columbus Day protests and other activities in their communities – these may not seem much of a match for a government-corporate enterprise which was given an initial $87m grant by Congress to turn the quincentenary into an affirmation of American-style freedom, democracy and justice. But the alternative Columbus[4] groups have the potential to mount a significant threat to the establishment agenda – not because of their numbers, and not because of their funding, but because, during a presidential election year, when neither political party will want to disturb the layers of mystification and amnesia spun round the national consciousness, the counter-quincentenary movement offers a way of looking at current and historical reality which challenges accepted notions and smelly orthodoxies.

The national reality

Increasingly, the national myth has fallen out of step with the national reality. The 'many' out of which came the 'one' nation have never included those marginalised by systemic racism – the blacks, the Hispanics, the Asians and the Native Americans. And whatever gains they had made in the era of civil rights, native rights and rebellion have been eroded by the politics and policies of the Reagan and Bush administrations. These have systematically devastated social programmes in the inner cities, training programmes for the unemployed, housing provisions and assistance for families with children, while engineering, at the same time, a massive transfer of wealth from everybody else to the already-rich.

Today, the US has the widest gap between rich and poor of any industrial nation, the widest in modern history. Census statistics show that the richest 2.5m Americans (the top 1 per cent) now receive as much income after taxes as the bottom 100 million (bottom 40 per cent). (In 1980 the top 1 per cent received half as much as the bottom 40 per cent). During 1982-9 the number of billionaires quintupled, while the number of children living in poverty increased by more than 2.1 million to 12 million, or one in five of the nation's children.

The inner cities have been hardest hit, and black America brought to the verge of catastrophe. Three times more likely to live in poverty than whites, blacks are twice as likely to be unemployed. White households have ten times as much wealth as black households and the black median income, which had been 61.3 per cent of the white median income in 1970, had declined by the mid-1980s to 55 per cent. Even the families which have made it into the 'middle class' – some one in seven of all black families – earn, on average, 50-70 per cent of what white middle-class families earn. A middle-class income does not shield them from discrimination in the workplace, in the housing market, or when dealing with financial institutions – and the police. Lacking substantial assets, most are only a few pay cheques away from poverty.

Among the Latino community, despite the large proportion of families with two working parents, one child in three now lives in poverty; Latino children accounted for half the increase in the total number of poor children during the decade. According to Census bureau data, 43 per cent of the increase in poverty between 1979 and 1989 was caused by federal, state and local reductions in government benefit programmes. A September 1991 report by the Washington-based Joint Center for Political and Economic Studies revealed that, in spite of the higher economic growth rates in the US in the 1980s, the US poverty rate was substantially higher than that of European industrial nations because its welfare system was so inadequate.

And criminalisation has followed close on the heels of immiseration. The majority of black families are as likely to see their children go to prison as college. One in four of black men between the ages of 20 and 29 is either in jail, or awaiting trial or on parole. The so-called war on drugs has been fought almost exclusively in black neighbourhoods, though 'drug czar' William Bennett acknowledged in 1989 that 'the typical cocaine user is white, a high school graduate employed full-time and living in a small metropolitan area or suburb'.[5] Despite the fact that only 12 per cent of black Americans (who make up 12 per cent overall of population) have been estimated to use drugs, the great majority of those arrested in major drug sweeps have been African-

American. By 1990, more than a million people had been arrested on drug charges and 'minority' offenders were twice as likely to get prison terms as young white males arrested on identical charges. During the last decade, the US doubled its prison population and moved from third place to head of the pack in the per capita rate at which it imprisons its citizens, locking up black males at a rate four times greater than South Africa. *[6]

At the same time, the political programmes, such as affirmative action, and political concepts, such as group remedies, which in the 1960s and 1970s had helped give minorities a semblance of an equal start in life, have been undermined by the Supreme Court rulings of 1989/90[7] which struck down methods used since the passage of the 1964 Civil Rights Act to fight employment discrimination against 'minorities' and women. These rulings have given the green light to more than 6,000 legal challenges to racial discrimination in the courts – brought by white men charging 'reverse discrimination'. There are currently twenty-five challenges to court-ordered consent decrees which have, over the past two decades, forced police and fire departments to hire women and 'minority' applicants. State and local government programmes that set aside a certain percentage of contracts for black- and Hispanic-owned businesses are being dismantled. Public interest law firms are now wary of mounting expensive discrimination cases, since they can no longer use statistics to prove a pattern of discrimination against a whole group, but must instead demonstrate in federal courts where half the judges are Reagan-appointees that discrimination against a particular plaintiff was 'intentional' on the part of an employer.

'Melting pot-ism' vs multiculturalism

But there is a cloud on the establishment horizon: the demographic balance of the US is changing 'at a breathtaking rate', according to the 1990 census. The 'minority' population, which was growing twice as fast during the 1980s as during the 1970s, now accounts for one-quarter of all Americans. Since 1980, the number of Hispanics in the US has risen by 50 per cent and the Asian-American population has doubled.

By 2050, it is predicted, Americans of European descent will be the new 'minority' nationwide; they are already a minority in states like California and New Mexico. The notion of the US as a 'melting pot' of

---

* Other statistics divide just as sharply on racial lines. The gap between life expectancy rates for whites and for blacks has grown wider every year since 1984. If they make it past childhood, residents of Bangladesh live longer than residents of Harlem: the US now ranks twenty-second in infant mortality.

European immigrants is being challenged by the sheer weight of demographic fact. And the presence of 'minority' children in the classroom (currently one in three; in thirty years one in two), and to a much lesser extent in higher education (some 16 per cent in colleges), is, of necessity, forcing the issue of multiculturalism and the real nature of American society on to the agenda.

Those who have read the signs argue that curricula must be revised so that students can recognise themselves in what they study. As the New York state social studies review and development committee stated in its June 1991 report, *One Nation, Many Peoples: a declaration of cultural interdependence*, 'multicultural education, anchored to the shared principles of a liberal democracy, is today less an educational innovation than a national priority'. It is 'necessary for the cultural health, social stability and economic future of New York state and the nation', since all citizens must believe 'that they and their ancestors have shared in building the country and a stake in its success'. It recommended 'seven guiding principles' for the social studies curriculum. One was 'democracy: bridging the gap between reality and the ideal'. Students should understand 'that the social, legal, and political struggles of disenfranchised people (for example, those who did not own property, people of color, women) to make America live up to its ideals have historically been potent forces strengthening and helping to expand the application of the Constitution'. Another was 'economic and social justice . . . Students should understand the importance of holding themselves and others accountable for promoting economic fairness and social justice'. Under 'globalism', it asked: 'How does the US interrelate with other nations . . . What forms has economic development taken around the world? What have been their consequences?'

But even before the proposed curriculum could get off the ground, the cry rose up that this was a project which was both un-American and unacceptable. * For most of this century, ever since a similar ideological crusade against immigrants and dangerous ideas culminating in the first 'red scare' after the First World War, it has been considered 'un-American' to look too closely at the existing economic system, power relations and social structures and to speak in terms of class. Early in the twentieth century, the fear that radicalism was being imported along with immigrants speaking strange languages led to the creation of 'Americanisation' programmes intended to instil proper patriotic principles. 'Americanisation day' on 4 July, 1915 bore the title 'Many peoples, one nation', inverted by this year's New York

---

* New York governor Mario Cuomo said that the furore could turn out to be bigger than the 1988 presidential election clamour over students refusing to stand for the pledge of allegiance.[8]

social studies review report. By 1919, fifteen states had decreed that English must be the only language of instruction in schools. Seventy years later, some seventeen states passed new 'English only' laws.

Today's onslaught against the 'culture of diversity' is intended to ensure that, if the curriculum is broadened to include new 'voices', evidence of 'minority' achievement and even 'multiple perspectives' as the multiculturalists demand, people will remain divided and ignorant of history, and social reality will be kept at bay. So that any multiculturalism which survives the right-wing offensive is intended to be weak and ineffectual, stripped of its analytic potential and power to mount an effective challenge to the status quo. It will be simply a way of 'managing diversity' without recognising the reality of racism. An 'effective multicultural school', in the words of a Massachusetts headmaster, 'will permit its members to interact both with an accurate knowledge of cultural differences and without awkward, distracting concerns about racism and prejudice'.[9] Anti-racism education, on the other hand, 'may precipitate concerns about social justice'.

Multiculturalism as political correctness

It is these self-same concerns, focused around issues of racism, sexism and homophobia, which have been agitating student minorities on the campuses. Synonymous with the struggle for multiculturalism and its 'enforcement arm', political correctness (PC), they have earned the opprobrium and sustained onslaught of the New Right. Pat Buchanan, former director of communications in the Reagan White House, summed up the New Right's position clearly in the August 1991 issue of his publication, *From the Right*. Declaring that there was 'a rising demand on campus for black studies, for black fraternities and multicultural education', Buchanan concluded by quoting an official from the American Immigration Control Foundation that 'the combined forces of open immigration and multiculturalism constitute a mortal threat to American Civilisation'.

This 'mortal threat' has been met by a formidably well-organised and well-funded campaign. For some years now, the New Right has been laying the groundwork for all-out combat over the issues of affirmative action and curriculum reform. Major New Right institutions like the Heritage Foundation and the Institute for Educational Affairs had, since the early Reagan years, been preparing a strategy to colonise the campuses, working through groups like Accuracy in Academia, which monitored what was being taught in college classrooms. Several members of its board and its president, John Le Boutillier, were also members of the World Anti-Communist League, which had close links with Latin American death-squads, nazi collaborators and Rev Sun Myung Moon.

In 1987, the National Association of Scholars was created to spearhead the attack against liberal ideas on campus. It had close ties with Reagan's education secretary later turned 'drug czar', William Bennett. It soon attracted more than 1,400 faculty members and, with its budget of $250,000, established a research centre, fellows programme, speakers bureau, state and regional affiliates and the quarterly journal *Academic Questions*.

Then, in 1988, came the Madison Center (with funding from Coors, Scaife, Mobil and other corporations) to promote the study of the 'major works of the western world'. In September 1990, the Center merged with the Institute for Educational Affairs, to form the Madison Center for Educational Affairs. More than sixty right-wing student publications, including the *Dartmouth Review* (notorious for its hounding of a black Dartmouth professor and for quoting Hitler on its masthead) came under its aegis. It also immediately began to promote its 'collegiate network' with a view to helping 'student publications overcome the substantial obstacles they continue to encounter while trying to wage the battle of ideas on campus'.[10] The network fosters the exchange of information and articles, and organises seminars and site visits by various luminaries of the New Right. It has its 'hotline' to discuss urgent problems, and a monthly newsletter, *Newslink*, which gives tips on story ideas, as well as the nationally syndicated *Collegiate Times*, which is sent to over 900 college newspapers. With the help of the Madison Center, student publications are assured of funding from advertisers like Coors. They are provided with copies of 'new and important books' and other information from 'a group we call CN friends' – including the National Review, the Heritage Foundation and the Hudson Institute. Student editors are given a glimpse of the future they can expect within the New Right family: 'One summer twenty Collegiate Network students were able to spend almost an hour with White House Chief of Staff John Sununu and President George Bush.'[11]

The Madison Center for Educational Affairs has made a special effort to organise black and Latino students into a Student Forum which would counter all attempts to increase ethnic diversity in academia. Under the direction of David Bernstein, who is half black and half Jewish, the Student Forum now has a monthly newsletter and syndicated column concentrating entirely on race issues.

As well as the Madison Center, the National Association of Scholars and Accuracy in Academia, right-wing ideologues also push their wares through College Republicans, which claims a membership of 100,000 and over 1,000 college chapters, and numerous other student organisations which are allied to the religious Right.

Through such agencies is the struggle against multiculturalism, actively expressed as PC, currently being waged. PC, a self-mocking term from the 1960s Left, is now construed as the new McCarthyism, pursuing an anti-white, anti-male, anti-heterosexist witch-hunt on the campus. With the 'evil empire' in ruins, the new life-and-death struggle for all patriotic Americans lies within its own classrooms and campuses. The Young America's Foundation newsletter for May 1991 told its members that 'black radical students and faculty, militant homosexuals, and far left political agitators' were taking over colleges by storm: 'Terrified by the fact that students are becoming more and more conservative, free speech, free and independent thought is being all but eliminated from American college campuses.'

In its 17 May newsletter, the *American Sentinel* saw things essentially the same way:

> The growing PC movement is the liberal response to the increasing popularity of conservative ideals on campus – especially among students who have rejected the failed ideology of socialism in favour of Ronald Reagan's agenda to lower taxes, promote equal opportunity and resist social engineering [i.e., affirmative action].

Outlining in lurid terms the activities of 'PC fascists' on campus, the newsletter asked its members to donate funds to defeat the 'liberal' plan to force universities to abandon merit for racial preferences.

And the major media were only too ready to engage in the shadow-boxing stage-managed by the New Right. While the Gulf war was laying to rest that spectre from the 1960s, the 'Vietnam syndrome', the major newspapers as well as *Newsweek, Time*, the entire February issue of the *New Republic*, the *Atlantic Monthly* (which turned over twenty-one pages of its March issue to the guru of the campus New Right, Dinesh D'Souza, * *Harper's, New York Review of Books, New York* magazine and *Tikkun* were, within a matter of months, taking up cudgels against PC. 'A growing emphasis on the nation's "multicultural" heritage exalts racial and ethnic pride at the expense of social cohesion', proclaimed the cover story of *Time* on 8 July 1991. 'The customs, beliefs, and principles that have unified the US, however imperfectly, for more than two centuries are being challenged with a ferocity not seen since the civil war.'

As portrayed in the media, the hearts, minds and books of 'western civilisation' are at stake in a frontal assault against tolerance, individual freedom, democracy and the belief in a 'common culture' – those traditional values that have kept the country together. The

---

* D'Souza, an immigrant from India, was a founder of the *Dartmouth Review* and later a domestic policy analyst at the Reagan White House. His writings have provided much of the ammunition for the attack on multicultural education and affirmative action. In recent months, his articles have appeared in publications ranging from the right-wing newsletter *Crisis* (April 1991) to the Spring 1991 *Social Studies Review* and the *New York Times* (7 July 1991).

assault has been mounted by the new tribalists, the high priests of the 'cult of multiculturalism'. Their agenda is (according to a *Wall Street Journal* headline) quite simply 'un-American'. Drawing their evidence from the anecdotes, distortions and fantasies found in D'Souza's *Illiberal Education: the politics of race and sex on campus*,[12] the media have depicted campuses as being under the sway of PC bullies, the shock troops of the 1960s who have infiltrated into positions of power in universities where they work to replace the western literary canon and 'Eurocentric' curricula with ethnic and feminist studies, and white professors with a 'diverse' faculty, no matter what this might mean for academic standards.

In all the furore over PC, the facts are immaterial: during the last decade, only a handful of colleges and universities have embarked on attempts to include 'multiple perspectives' in the teaching of history and literature, more black studies departments have been eliminated than courses on Shakespeare, and only 2 per cent of faculty members at major universities are black.

The facts are also immaterial when the media and George Bush lament the 'rise of intolerance in our land'. In his speech on 4 May 1991 at the University of Michigan graduation ceremony, Bush elevated PC to the status of national bogey, an enemy to both free speech and racial harmony. He made no mention of the growing number of racial attacks and acts of everyday harassment which led some 200 colleges by the spring of 1991 to adopt codes of behaviour and speech in an effort to restore civility to campus life, Instead it is 'the PC brigade' which has made universities hostile territory for students who are not white by bullying students who are, setting up 'inquisitions' to control what they think and say in violation of the First Amendment. It is the PC brigade which is responsible for the high failure and drop-out rates of black students, by insisting that they are admitted in the first place. If racism does exist on campus, it is PC which has actively nurtured it. In the name of diversity, students who are not qualified have been encouraged to enter university, where they take refuge from their own inadequacies by withdrawing into their own ethnic groups, and spend their time bitterly attacking the 'racism' of their fellow students.

Giving hostages to the Right

The battle over PC has been a largely one-sided contest. In most of the academic world, progressive forces seem both fragmented and paralysed; fragmented by the all-consuming politics of identity into abstract and apolitical categories of 'culture' and oppression, and paralysed by a fixation on texts, language and the self, and the search for 'self-esteem'.

This has not always been the case. Vincent Harding has written eloquently of the way the movement for black studies, 'which paved the way for an expanded multicultural educational vision of America', was rooted in the 'freedom/justice movement' of the 1950s and 1960s and the demands made by hundreds of local communities for a role in defining their own past, their present and their future. They attempted 'to open the arena, to say that there is more to American history than white-defined history, more to American literature than white-established canons, more to "the American people" than a collection of blond and blue-eyed Norman Rockwell creations'.[13] Just as the women's movement and movement for gay rights grew out of the civil rights movement, so demands for women's studies and gay studies followed the successful establishment of black studies departments.

By the late 1970s, all these movements to 'revision' American education had become detached from any political context. There was no movement any more. For reasons described by Jenny Bourne, there was only a consciousness of oppression:

> Oppression became the new political yardstick. Everyone was oppressed or oppressing – men of women, whites of blacks, heterosexuals of homosexuals, Christians of Jews. A friend could oppress with a joke . . . The distinction between idea and act, between individual and structure, between the real world and its representation was completely lost. And the way to fight oppression was not so much to challenge power directly as to challenge discourse, the mode in which power relations are discussed and represented.[14]

One challenged discourse by breaking it down, taking texts apart to examine components for racial, cultural and gender biases. And, in the process, everything is broken into constituent parts, including the very notion of community and of a unifying political culture. The preoccupation with self and personal identity has led to a fracturing into smaller and smaller cliques of the similarly oppressed. Colleges have separate groups for lesbians of colour and white lesbians; gay men of colour and gay white men. If the *New Republic* is to be believed, *The Dictionary of Cautionary Words and Phrases* produced by the Multicultural Management Program Fellows defines 'community' this way: 'Implies a monolithic culture in which people act, think, and vote in the same way. Do not use, as in Asian, Hispanic, black or gay community. Be more specific as to what the group is, e.g. black residents in a northside neighborhood.'[15]

Today, there is a hollow confusion at the core of what remains of a progressive campus movement, a measure of the extent to which it has been disconnected from reality, from an understanding of the economic and ideological forces shaping the world and of what it will take to change them. Historically hamstrung by a lack of class analysis, progressives have, in the last decade or so, been further impoverished by the amnesia which has cut them off from the freedom movement of the 1950s and 1960s, and the struggles for democracy which it inspired. The battle against 'racism' has turned inward, becoming simultaneously personal and abstract, to be fought in sensitivity workshops and decoded in the words of the white men who personalise prejudice and the power to oppress.

Forgotten is the lesson which Martin Luther King learned late in his life. At a staff retreat in November 1966, he admitted that the civil rights movement had made only surface changes, which had left the roots of racism virtually untouched. In its next stage, King argued, the movement would have to pursue 'substantive' changes and would 'be making demands that will cost the nation something' because they would be raising 'class issues – issues that relate to the privileged as over against the underprivileged'. The heart of the matter, King finally saw clearly, was that 'something is wrong with the economic system of our nation . . . something is wrong with capitalism'.[16]

With the killing of King and the death of the Black Power movement, the nation has been spared these demands. Since then, the insights which Martin Luther King came to share with Malcolm X have been deliberately erased from public understanding. During the late 1960s and 1970s, the neoconservatives, many of them prominent Jewish intellectuals willing to overlook the association of Republican Party officials with known nazi collaborators, mounted an offensive against the Black Power movement, viewing it as a threat to both law and order and democratic pluralism. By the late 1970s, they had broadened their attack to include affirmative action (defined as 'reverse discrimination' by the time of the 1978 Bakke case) and the concept of institutional racism. Racism, when seen as more than a black complaint, was made interchangeable with bigotry. Both were a matter of personal attitudes, to be confronted on the purely personal level.

To show how, the Anti-Defamation League of B'nai B'rith produced a curriculum for schools which has been widely circulated, *A World of Difference: a prejudice reduction program* (1985). Featuring a letter from Ronald Reagan as its preface, the curriculum defined prejudice as 'an attitude in a closed mind', discrimination as 'leaving somebody out because of prejudiced thinking' and racism as coupling 'the false assumption that race determines psychology and cultural traits with the belief that one race is superior to another'. Society never enters the picture.

By the late 1980s, the entire ideological spectrum of the nation had moved so far to the right that no one was discerning a pattern in the practices which confined black children to increasingly segregated and run-down schools in neighbourhoods demarcated by 'redlining',* in the paramilitary style of policing inner city ghettoes, in the targeting of black elected officials by the FBI, in the judicial decisions about who gets condemned to death and for what crimes, or in the difference in life expectancy rates between black and white, and the unwavering facts about who is last to be hired and first to be laid off. African-Americans, whose long collective struggle had provided an alternative to the fragmenting individualism of America, had to be brought into line and given a leadership acceptable to the Right. The task of discrediting affirmative action was, by the late 1980s, being spear-headed by a small group of black neoconservatives and was intended both to divide the black population and to discredit the very notion of community, of collective struggles and group remedies.

Shelby Steele, author of the lavishly praised *The Content of Our Character: a new vision of race in America* (1990), is one who has given the Right what it wants to hear. Steele writes not of racism but of white guilt, black anxiety and inadequacy, the need for uplift and a loss of memory. Blacks are oppressed today, Steele states, by the collective memory of racism, 'the irresistible pull into the past' which can 'render opportunities in the present all but invisible'.[17] Preoccupied with their collective identity, African-Americans have neglected to develop themselves as individuals:

> To retrieve our individuality and find opportunity, blacks today must – consciously or unconsciously – disregard the prevailing victim-focused black identity. Though it espouses black pride, it is actually a repressive identity that generates a victimised self-image, curbs individualism and initiative, diminishes our sense of possibility, and contributes to our demoralisation and inertia.

How can black Americans change their condition? 'There will be no end to despair and no lasting solution to any of our problems until we rely on individual effort within the American mainstream – rather than collective action against the mainstream – as our means of advancement . . . The nexus of this new identity must be a meeting of black individual initiative and American possibility.' Its incarnation is Clarence Thomas.

Clarence Thomas, elevated to the US Supreme Court despite the fact that he only had seventeen months judicial experience, first came to national notice when he used his sister as an example of what was wrong with the welfare system at a major gathering of black neoconservatives in San Francisco in 1980. 'She gets mad when the mailman is late with her welfare check', Thomas told his audience. 'That's how

---

* 'Redlining' is the practice whereby banks restrict the mortgages they grant black applicants to certain areas.

dependent she is.' His sister had, in fact, worked at two jobs simultaneously to support her three children after being deserted by her husband. It was only when she had to look after an aunt who suffered a stroke that she went on welfare. She is now a cook at a hospital, and starts her working day each morning at 3am.[18]

Thomas's appointment to the Supreme Court on the grounds that he is 'the best man for the job on the merits' (as George Bush put it) is no less cynical than his own use of his sister to advance his personal standing within neoconservative circles. Alongside chief-of-staff Colin Powell, black Americans now have as a leading 'role model' a late twentieth-century Booker T. Washington and self-professed admirer of J.A. Parker.[19]

Parker, the first black member of the right-wing Young Americans for Freedom, has also been a member of the World Anti Communist League, and a founder of the Black Political Action Committee, which campaigned for the far-Right southern senator Jesse Helms in 1984. From 1977, Parker served as a lobbyist for South Africa. According to a South African newspaper report in 1988, he was receiving a yearly grant from Pretoria of $360,000. Parker is also president of a black think-tank, the Lincoln Institute for Research and Education, and editor of the *Lincoln Review*, which has consistently attacked Martin Luther King, the African National Congress, sanctions against South Africa, affirmative action and the notion that government pro-grammes can ameliorate social problems. Clarence Thomas joined the editorial board of the *Lincoln Review* in 1981, and was still a member of it a decade later.

Thomas, in fact, would fit the 'American dream' to perfection, except that his bootstraps were supplied by affirmative action. And yet, he is notorious for his attacks on the very concept of group remedies. Who more apt to complete and sustain the reversal of affirmative action policies than the man who rose through them? What better symbol to give credence to the myth of national unity and equality, as the nation becomes ever more fragmented and unequal?

Conclusion

With their reaffirmation of past mythologies, what the Columbus celebrations have done is to expose the divisions in American society and polarise the argument about its nature. Yet, they offer too an opportunity. At a time when the Right seems bent on rewriting not just the past but the present, on eradicating even the remembrance of collective action, let alone the lessons to be drawn from it, the quincentenary provides a rare chance to anchor culturalism and ethnicity to a history of collective struggle. 'Perhaps the approaching celebration of the five-hundredth anniversary could help turn things around', writes Eduardo Galeano, 'so topsy-turvy are they now. Not to confirm the world, adding to the self-importance, the self-glorification of the masters of power, but to denounce and change it. For that we shall have to celebrate the vanquished, not the victors.'[20]

'Columbus' as envisaged by Galeano and the groups mobilising for 1992 is about the face of 'western civilisation' which never makes it into the canon of the New Right. It is about capitalism, colonialism, racism, greed and resistance – everything which has been deemed off limits in political discourse. 1992 will succeed as a 'teachable moment' if it confronts the history of the 'first encounter' and its deadly aftermath in all its fullness, not just the myths and realities of 'discovery', but of capitalism itself and the ways it has been and is still served by racism. 'Columbus' has the potential to reconstruct the relationship between oppression and history and to connect education with the world beyond ideology and the self, the world of current reality. It offers a way to span the centuries, allowing students to discover that, as Dr Jeane Sindab of the World Council of Churches told an alternative quincentary meeting in Brazil, 'the same greedy drive for profit and the accumulation of capital which was the impetus for 1492 still shapes the political, economic, and social parameters of our existence, as we head toward 1992'.[21]

What is the likelihood of this sort of education, anathema to the New Right, making it into the classroom? Thanks to the spread of multiculturalism, with its stress on diverse voices and multiple perspectives which the New Right has not yet succeeded in reversing, it might be difficult to keep it out.

The 'view from the shore' can bring to multiculturalism a new sense of what racism is, and transform it into an anti-racist education which helps students know not just 'who they are', but why things are the way they are. It can introduce the sort of questions which are rarely voiced in schools or presidential election campaigns.

'Why do such enormous inequities of wealth and power exist in the world and within the United States? What might be the economic/political interests of some people for keeping some communities more wealthy than others?'[22] These questions, so alien to multiculturalism as it is generally conceived but prefigured in the recommended curriculum changes in New York, currently appear on worksheets created for seventh-graders in Oakland, California, by teachers who rejected a new textbook purporting to be multicultural. Other sections examine why toxic waste dumps are put mainly in poor neighbourhoods and how racial stereotypes are perpetuated. Public pressure generated by media attention forced the teachers to abandon a section called 'Crimes of a racist society', which featured a cartoon of Clarence Thomas. The various alternative Columbus curricula which groups of teachers around the country are presently assembling should find a receptive audience in this Oakland school.[23]

If the alternative quincentenary can bring clarity to what is now obscure and, in so doing, help 'turn things around', it will not come a moment too soon. For the Columbus of the official jubilee celebrations masks rapid strides towards what Bertram Gross more than a decade ago gave the name 'friendly fascism' – a concentrated, impersonal big business/big government partnership designed to perpetuate advanced capitalism and the profits and privileges of the 'ultra' rich, sustained by the manipulation of myths and legitimised by hollow democratic processes. In the United States, it would 'be supermodern and multi-ethnic – as American as Madison Avenue, executive luncheons, credit cards and apple pie. It would be fascism with a smile.'[24]

1 Telephone conversation (13 September 1991).
2 BBC TV, channel 2, 'Late show special' (10 October 1991).
3 Columbus Quincentenary Jubilee Convention, official brochure.
4 For a list of organisations involved in alternative Columbus activities, see *Rethinking Schools* (October/November 1990), which is available from 1001 East Keefe Avenue, Milwaukee, WI 53212, or the successive issues of *Huracan*, a publication of the Alliance for Cultural Democracy, PO Box 7591, Minneapolis, MN 55407.
5 'A national drug control strategy' (Washington, *The White House*, September 1989).
6 Marc Mauer, *Americans Behind Bars: a comparison of international rates of incarceration* (The Sentencing Project, January 1991).
7 The Supreme Court rulings rolling back the gains of the civil rights movement are described in Louis Kushnick, 'US: the revocation of civil rights' in *Race & Class* (July-September 1990). Affirmative action is grounded in Title VII of the Civil Rights Act of 1964: 'It shall be unlawful employment practice for an employer to fail or refuse to hire or to discharge an individual because of such an individual's race, colour, religion, sex or national origin.' Southern legislators had added 'sex' to the list in a vain attempt to prevent it from passing. White women have been the primary beneficiaries of affirmative action practices.
8 *Education Week* (31 July, 1991).
9 *Milton Magazine* (Summer 1990).
10 From the Collegiate Network's informational brochure. This and other news-letters of the Right were made available by Political Research Associates, an independent research organisation in Cambridge, Massachusetts, which collects and disseminates information on right-wing political groups and trends.
11 Press release announcing the formation of the Madison Centre for Educational Affairs.
12 Dinesh D'Souza, *Illiberal Education: the politics of race and sex on campus* (New York, 1991).
13 Vincent Harding, *Hope and History: why we must share the story of the movement* (New York, 1990), pp.40-41.
14 Jenny Bourne, *Homelands of the Mind: Jewish feminism and Identity Politics* (London, IRR, 1987), p.3.

15   *New Republic* (18 February 1991).
16   Quoted in D. Garrow, *Bearing the Cross: Martin Luther King and the Southern Christian Leadership Conference* (New York, 1986) p. 537.
17   Shelby Steele, *The Content of Our Character* (New York, 1990) pp. 151-2.
18   *New York Times* 23 July 1991.
19   Clarence Thomas, 'Why black Americans should look to conservative policies', a speech delivered to the Heritage Foundation (18 June 1987).
20   Eduardo Galeano, 'The Blue Tiger and the Promised Land' in *Report on the Americas: inventing America, 1492-1992* (NACLA, February 1991), p.17.
21   Dr Jeane Sindab, 'Blacks, Indigenous People and the Churches: 1992, ending the pain, beginning the hope', background paper for Continental Consultation on Racism in the Americas, 23-29 September, 1990, Rio de Janeiro, Brazil.
22   *New York Times* (19 September 1991).
23   One of the most promising of these is *Rethinking Columbus*, a curriculum being produced by *Rethinking Schools* in collaboration with the Network of Educators on Central America. It can be ordered in bulk from *Rethinking Schools*, address above.
24   Bertram Gross, *Friendly Fascism* (Boston, South End Press, 1980), p.3.

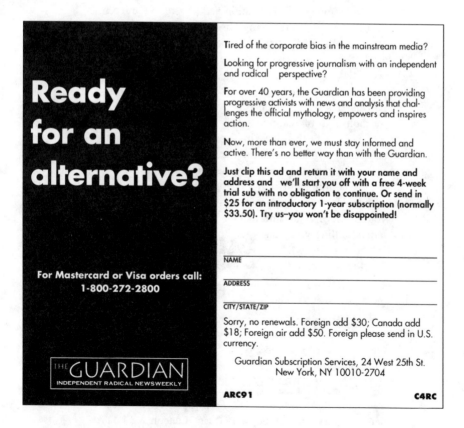

STOP
CIVILISATION

(£ ONLY 12)

In the name of civilisation and progress, the lives of tribal people·are being threatened. Their homes are demolished, their land taken away. Rainforests are bulldozed and rivers polluted. All these things are done illegally.

These tribes don't want charity, clothing or food parcels. They have lived peaceful, self-sufficient lives for thousands of years.

They do need voices, like yours, to join their own in combating big business, the banks and corrupt governments that threaten to destroy their right to a future.

To continue the fight for tribal rights, we depend on membership, not government subsidy. As a member, you will receive an information pack and regular newsletters, telling you what has been achieved. Please join now.

Survival
for tribal peoples

Name_____

Address_____

_____

I enclose a cheque/postal order for £12 ☐   £3 ☐ (concessionary)

Please charge my Access/Visa/Mastercard to:

Signature:_____ Expiry date:_____

Send to: Survival, 310 Edgware Road, London W2 1DY.

Founded 1969. President: Robin Hanbury-Tenison O.B.E. Director General: Stephen Corry.
Registered Charity 267444. Company Registration 1056317. Tel: 071 723 5535; Fax: 071 723 4059.

CHRIS SEARLE

Unlearning Columbus: a review article

As the nautical writer John Dyson puts it in his celebratory volume,
Columbus: for gold, God and glory[1], 'After Jesus Christ, no individual
has made a bigger impact upon the Western world than Christopher
Columbus.' Five hundred years after his fateful landfall on Guanahani
island, in 1992, he even threatens to overtake the one in the lead.

So perhaps when dealing with such a totemic figure in history,
every reviewer should give a brief autobiographical glimpse into their
encounter with those such as Columbus whose followers have made
bigger than history itself, their introduction and sustenance into the
myth and the monument. For children such as I was, growing up
unconsciously in the mind's eye of British imperialism in the years
immediately before its formal disintegration and the detachment of its
colonies after decades of struggle by those who were its subjects,
Columbus represented its pioneer and foundation.

Who knew him as the much more sinister 'Colon' – that ominous
homophone for colony? Who knew what a 'colony' actually was,
beyond an extension of Britain (with the bigger ones providing cricket
teams to play against us), a portion of the world where, despite the
climate, the jungle and deserts, disease and poverty, the people at
least tried to do things in the British way and were thankful to us for it.
And this was what linked us to Columbus. British history generally
does not like foreigners (unless they are Americans), but yet it always
seemed to like Columbus, seemed to see him almost as a special kind

Chris Searle is a writer and teacher working in Sheffield. His most recent book is *A
Blindfold Removed: Ethiopia's struggle for literacy* (London, Karia Press, 1991).

Race & Class, 33, 3 (1992)

of Englishman. At school – he 'discovered' America: it was unambiguous, it did not matter if anyone else lived there or had arrived there
before he came. There was no doubt about it: he, and he alone,
'discovered' America. There were some marginal stories about Leif
Ericson and his Vikings or Egyptians in paper boats, but Columbus
never had a real challenger. It was he who had discovered that the
world was round, nobody else was ever considered. It was he who had
persuaded the sensible and humane Queen Isabella of Spain to pawn
her jewels to pay for his voyage – and we learned about his triumphs to
the chorus of a sentimental song played time after time over the radio
of the mid-1950s, which ended with the winsome line naming the tiny
ships that carried him and his men across an ocean that was to become
a crossing of agony and death, 'The *Pinta*, the *Niña* . . . and the *Santa
Mar . . . i . . . a!*'

In the secondary modern school I went to, we put on a play about
the life of Columbus. The role of honour went to the first student the
school had ever produced who had gained five 'O' levels. 'Look at him
now', the teachers said to us as he played his character on the stage of
the school hall with ruff, frock coat and black stockings, surrounded
by bemused sailors as he stood an egg on its end, 'You can also do well
and be like him.' So he was more than an exemplary man of history, he
was an institution. And Columbus also became our aspiration, he was
there for us to emulate.

It was all this that later we had somehow to unlearn, and the
unlearning was a powerful enough task. For me, a black American
started this process in my suburban London home. As a teenager, I
began a lifelong love of jazz, and my particular favourite artist was the
nonpareil of stride piano and musical humour, Thomas 'Fats' Waller.
In April 1936, in a New York studio, Waller and his sidemen had
recorded a tongue-in-cheek version of the novelty song of the period
(written by Andy Razaf, himself a Madagascan by birth), *Christopher
Columbus*. In the unlikely lyrics, Columbus – sailing with no aid to
direction – quells a mutiny on board the *Santa Maria* by using 'rhythm
as a compass'. Then, after some of the hottest music that Waller and
his men ever put together on wax, the comical banter changes
suddenly to a caustic unaccompanied sentence at the end of the
record. Parodying the lines by the American Winifred Sackville
Stoner Jr that every schoolchild learns, and adding his own tailpiece,
Waller chants:

> In fourteen hundred and ninety-two
> Columbus sailed the ocean blue –
> What happened?

These last two words, said so bitterly by a man whose voice carried so
much public laughter, stayed with me, always returning for years after

when I encountered the real America. What did they mean? What was he saying? They came back nearly a decade later when I climbed up the great pre-Columbian pyramids of Teotihuacan, just outside Mexico City, and I thought out loud – who could ever say they discovered these except those who built them? They came back when, as a schoolteacher in the Caribbean island of Tobago – which Columbus had skirted in 1498 after passing through the Gulf of Paria and seeing the American mainland for the first time during his third voyage – I was shown the collection of Arawak artifacts that an archaeologist friend from Trinidad had disinterred from the island's beaches. What other human being can discover what is *already* of humans? For Columbus had come as an outvoyager of the system that did not discover without appropriating, did not find without keeping and enslaving.

So, in reading these books new for 1992, and offering reviews, my criteria retain the clarity of that early unlearning. For what was I to learn later of this voyager and 'discoverer'? That, as a citizen of Genoa, he emblematised the dedication inscribed on every Genoese ledger: 'In the name of God and profit', and carried with him the 'shameless' epithet that Dante ascribed to the materialistic and venal values that characterised that maritime republic. He was the man so tight-fisted as to deny the promised reward to the seaman on the *Pinta*, Juan Rodriguez, for the first to see the 'new' land in the west on the first voyage, keeping the money for himself after claiming that he had seen the same land the evening before. He was the instigator of transatlantic slavery, who shackled to his deck six unsuspecting Taino people after the first landfall on the Bahamas in 1492, eventually carrying them back to Spain. He was the prototypal colonist who first 'pacified' the Caribbean by countenancing the *encomienda* allocation of slaves to settlers, and oversaw the erection of 340 sets of gallows across the island of 'Hispaniola'. He was the self-proclaimed 'messenger of a new heaven' whose brief rule as a governor of the same island accounted for the deaths of some 50,000 of its people, whose lust for gold and profit made him decree that every Taino man, woman and child over the age of 14 must deliver, every three months, a hawk's bell crammed with gold – those who failed were to be hanged in groups of thirteen, 'in memory of Our Redeemer and His twelve apostles'. It was this man that we had been taught to admire in our days at school. And, for me, this was the beginning of the answer to Fats Waller's rhetorical question of 1936: 'what happened?'

Considering these things in 1991, following a bloody war for oil on the shores of the Persian Gulf, it is almost as if we can substitute that twentieth-century mineral for its fifteenth-century progenitor. For it was Columbus, anticipating George Bush and his oil-lust, who wrote (in the logbook of his first voyage): 'Of gold is treasure made, and with it he who has it does as he wills in the world and even sends souls to Paradise.' And it was a Nahuatl commentator who, beholding the behaviour of the invaders of the 'new world' that was his country, perhaps foretold the response of Arab peoples to the oil-conquistadors of 1991:

> They lifted up the gold as if they were monkeys, with expressions of joy, as if it put new life into them and lit up their hearts. As if it were certainly something for which they yearn with a great thirst. Their bodies fatten on it and they hunger violently for it. They crave gold like hungry swine.

For our teachers and our schools the tasks of learning and unlearning, both 1492 and 1991, have never been greater.

An instructive place to start is in the historical fiction of the Mexican poet and novelist, Homero Aridjis, whose *1492: the life and times of Juan Cabezon*[2] reveals the seedbed of Columbus's projects and the successive growth of European imperialism. For where did Columbus find the money to finance his enterprise? Certainly, some came from Genoese and Florentine merchants – and the cost of two of his ships was levied against the seaport town of Palos from where he set sail. But the balance came from the crown, and who filled the coffers of the crown, and how? In this masterpiece of historical narration, Aridjis tells us. The Inquisition, established by Queen Isabella and King Ferdinand after their persuasion had warmed the Pope, offered an effective and secure means of raising large amounts of money from Spanish Jewry and the new *conversos*, who switched religious allegiance in order to escape its reign of torture, ruin and death.

Aridjis' novel is about this fifteenth-century holocaust. 1492 was also the year of the Decree of Expulsion of all Jews from Spain and the expropriation of their property and wealth – with all goods and monies going to the king's exchequer to pay for the war against the Moors in southern Spain, and to underwrite the Atlantic voyages of 'discovery'. He shows, in the sweeping and indignant burst of the historical imagination which is his novel, the agony and genocidal terror that was this collecting – making clear how racism begat colonialism, which begat racism and imperialism. His picaresque protagonist, Juan Cabezon, moves through these events – the raids, the arrests, the racist humiliations, the public executions and burning horror of the *auto-da-fé*, the flight for life. Nothing could serve as a more profound and detailed prophecy of the political terror of our own century, from Auschwitz to Santiago, from My Lai to Soweto.

Halfway through the novel, Cabezon, fleeing from the familiars of the Inquisition, overhears a conversation between 'a navigator' and an agent of the Holy Office in a Toledo hostelry. The seaman claims to know 'how to reach the Indies by going west'. It is a transient, one page-long encounter, but enough to persuade Cabezon. At the end of the novel, he joins Columbus at Palos, ready to be a mastman on the *Santa Maria*.

In July 1990, an 'authentic replica' of the *Niña*, crewed by a Spanish professor of nautical studies and his students, retraced Columbus's original voyage in a prelude to the trans-oceanic spectacles that will arrive with the quincentenary. This crossing is fully documented, with dozens of full colour plates on high-quality shiny paper in *Columbus: for gold, God and glory*, with text by John Dyson and photographs by Peter Christopher. Alongside the images of the new voyage are maps, archival paintings of the Columbus era, charts and original illustrations that lie uneasily with the cinematic quality of the contemporary photographs – which are more about glory than gold or God. The reader must ask: why spend this money, go to these lengths, photograph so heroically and represent so admiringly this re-sailing of a journey that was so doom-laden for so many millions? Why have the same powerful publishing houses not committed the same resources and finance to a book of similar physical quality showing to the world the vibrant life, order and beauty which Columbus's landfall despoiled and destroyed – particularly when much of the text of this present book so strongly emphasises Columbus's profit-lust and stands as contradictory evidence within the 'glory' of the colour plates?

Dyson's main theme is that Columbus (the original Mr Ten per cent, who demanded of King Ferdinand that proportion of any riches he found on his expeditions) had a secret map. This, asserts Dyson, he probably stole from a shipwrecked sailor whom he met while living on the bleak Atlantic island of Porto Santo off Madeira, between 1477 and 1479. This map enabled Columbus to know exactly where he was going in 1492: 'His goal was not to find a new way to the Orient: he was on the hunt for gold.' Although this seems to square with what we know about the character of the 'great navigator', it is yet another story to add to the Columbus apocrypha. Dyson makes it sound very plausible though, and also gives a strong reminder of how Columbus interrupted his first historic voyage and spent some time with his mistress Doña Beatriz at the Canary island of Gomero, before he set sail again westwards. There he could see at first hand what Spanish colonialism had already done to the Guanches, the aboriginal people of the Canaries – which presaged his own work, yet to be done in the Caribbean: 'This Spanish style of colonialism by conquest, in which native people were enslaved or slaughtered, proved to be a dress rehearsal for what would come on a very much wider scale on the other side of the ocean.'

In the introduction to Hans Koning's essential *Columbus: his enterprise*,[3] the author reminds us how young people have for years

called for a revaluation of Columbus and his projects: 'A new
generation of children – black, white, red, yellow – in our schools has
been asking for a more objective, less Eurocentric, white race-
oriented teaching of history.' He is absolutely right, and if this book is
introduced to them, they will begin to get it very effectively through its
finely written pages. It is certainly a book written for young readers, to
set in motion a process of demystifying Columbus and the 'false
heroisms' that he represents, for 'the year 1492 opened an era of
genocide, cruelty and slavery on a larger scale than had ever been seen
before', and very few of us ever learned that in our schools. Profiteer,
Christian bigot, whose lasting dream was to find a westward entry to
carry the reconquest of Jerusalem from the Arab peoples, and who
made it as far as the Caribbean 'because he was the first captain to
steer far enough south to pick up the north-east tradewinds', Columbus saw nothing except through the lens of acquisition. Among his
first recorded words upon seeing the people of the Caribbean were,
'they would make fine servants'. Soon his compatriots would be
treating them, as the priest de las Casas described it, 'like the
excrement in a public square', while they were hanged on their own
fruit trees and slaughtered in their thousands by Toledo steel and their
own suicidal concoctions of cassava poison.

Koning's book is a rare achievement in the way in which its style
and content connect with the curiosity of young students, and can
dissipate the layers of lies and glorification that surround Columbus's
life and projects. It concludes with an interview with the Bolivian
political activist and writer, Domitila Chungara, author of the unfor-
gettable testimony of Columbus's legacy, *Let Me Speak*! She shows
how his life-quest for gold and profit still lives on to damn the lives of
those original peoples of the Americas who have survived. Columbus
in a new guise: 'We know that Latin America lies within the orbit of
foreign interests, of the International Monetary Fund, the multinationals, North American imperialism, all of which have an interest
in looting even greater riches.'

Even before the quincentenary has begun, at the time of writing
(September 1991) the first edition of Felipe Fernandez-Armesto's
Columbus,[4] is already out of print. It is clearly being seen as an
influential, possibly definitive, portrait of the man and explorer which
will be widely read during the commemorative year. This biography
again emphasises Columbus's appetite for profit and his assiduous
attempts to create his own historical persona and thereby become 'the
author of his own legend'. Yet Fernandez-Armesto, with all his
professorial authority (he is general editor of *The Times Atlas of World
Exploration* and director-designate of the Oxford comparative colonial history project), adds his own weight to the received myth,
portraying the 'weaver's son who rose to greatness' (as announced on

the flyleaf), as directly and personally responsible for the 'unique achievement – the discovery of America.'

Yet, later in the biography, he qualifies this significantly: Columbus is, in fact, '*our* discoverer of America' – Europe's man. And it is this naked Eurocentrism and open scorn of the pre-Columbian Americas and their peoples that makes the overall emphasis of the book backward and dubious – also suggesting that, in the European mercantilist tradition that was to follow, Columbus's profit-obsession was no bad thing. A good biography for a Thatcherite and post-Thatcherite age, this. Columbus pioneered to 'put a girdle round the Earth', declares Fernandez-Armesto, as if that was itself a global achievement rather than an imperial cord. He writes glowingly of Columbus making the Atlantic a 'European lake', as if he already had in his mind a pre-vision of NATO. And as for the peoples of the lands he encountered, they – against the 'peace-loving and biddable' prospects which Columbus saw in them – in fact only turned out to be 'shifty and deadly'. For Fernandez-Armesto, like his formidable subject, the Caribbean is characterised as 'cannibal country'. His comments – which do nothing to set aside the sordid colonial myth of Caribbean cannibalism invented by Columbus and his despoliation of the word 'Carib' to make it synonymous with the eating of human flesh – provoke an instant re-reading of the brilliant essay by the Barbadian-Harlem writer, Richard B. Moore, 'Caribs, Cannibals and Human Relations', which debunks the degradation of the original Caribbean people continued by an eminent Columbus scholar, 500 years after it was begun by Columbus himself.

Kirkpatrick Sale's *The Conquest of Paradise*[5] makes a very different approach to Columbus, concerning itself as much with the huge impact of his wake, as with his life and times. This is made very clear on the same key subject of 'cannibalism', in which Sale leaves Fernandez-Armesto's Columbian attitudes well behind. 'The myths surrounding the Caribs are almost entirely fabrications born in the fable-hearted mind of Cristobal Colon', declares Sale after presenting his evidence – and there is much else that is brave, true and myth-breaking in his outstanding book.

He sees Columbus's enterprise as the first project that sought to impose Europe upon a continent that was nothing but its own: 'It wasn't so much that Europe *discovered* America as that it *incorporated* it.' Sale's thematic stress upon Columbus as the man, who, as he continually testified in his journals, arrived to 'discover and acquire' (thus making the two words synonymous throughout his life's work), flaunting his preoccupation – as expressed in his letter to Queen Isabella – with 'things of great profit', makes his book effectively an examination of the base of imperialism. For 'only Europe was so interested in global dominance', and Sale presents a taxonomy of its crimes without jargon or sensationalism. He is particularly strong on showing the environmental devastation imposed upon America and its people as a direct result of Columbus's intervention as well as the destructive work of those who came after him, and its relationship to the ecological damage that had already been committed in Europe – such as the demolition of thousands of acres of forestlands. *The Conquest of Paradise* will remain a seminal text well after the quincentenary, demonstrating in an engagingly clear and often poetic style how all the worst structures and routines of the European mind and culture – from a savage frenzy of organised religious hatred, a predilection for exploiting the 'gentleness' of generous hosts to the habit of systematically destroying the balance and bounty of the natural environment – were all foisted upon the lands that, after Columbus and his associates, became the Americas.

> I'm searching for America, and I fear I won't find her
> . . . I'm calling America but she doesn't reply;
> those who fear the truth have hidden her.

Thus wrote Panamanian poet Ruben Blades in his poem *Looking for America*, which is quoted by Duncan Green in his unremitting survey of the contemporary inheritance of Columbus's 1492 landfall, *Faces of Latin America*.[6]

Green has done a most useful service in compiling his book at this particular time and date, for it stands as a concise and compact amalgam of facts and commentary upon Latin America today, and the ways in which the region's condition reaches directly back to Columbus and his historic moment. For what came after – as soon as Columbus set about building his first colony at the 'Isabella' settlement on the northern coast of 'Hispaniola', institutionalising the subjugation of the local peoples and their hospitable *cacique*, Guacanagari – was the creation of, in Green's words, 'the most unequal continent in the world'. His book is a grotesque but factual journey through the many different dimensions of this horrific inequality as they are manifested today. From the narco-capitalism of Peru and Colombia, which continues to enslave eight million consumers in the US alone, it runs through the environmental disasters of places like the Brazilian city of Cubatao, where deadly toxic dioxanes and benzene produced and dumped by foreign multinationals have caused so many people to die and lives to be wrecked ('We are being forced to choose between poverty and poison', declared one campaigner), to the hamburger imperialism providing for the US fast-food market which is denuding the Central American states of erstwhile healthy farming and ranching lands. All this, and the grim tyrannies and autocracies that sustain it through many parts of the Americas, is the flotsam and jetsam of the *Santa Maria* and her little flotilla, the consequences of Columbus's four mortal voyages.

The Voice of the Victims, 1492-1992 [7] raises the question of whether any authentic Christian could ever feel sanguine about Columbus's 1492 arrival and its ensuing 500 years. 'It is not the memory of a blessing, but the nightmare of a genocide', write the editors, Virgil Elizondo and Leonardo Boff, in their introductory essay. The contributors write in awe of what their predecessors from Europe have done and what continues to happen for the sake of US and European expansionism, including 'extinguishing, snuffing out thousands of peoples with their original languages and cultures, and exterminating at least three great civilizations'. Thus, a sustained note of overwhelming guilt envelops the articles that form this book.

Yet, in the tradition of de las Casas, there is a sharp and compassionate witness to be found in the authors' words. They hold up no spiritual illusions to conceal, only the reality of the experience of the victims to reveal. And not just the victims, but those who struggle and organise too. Reminiscent of las Casas' recounting of the aims of Columbus and his company's Christian mission – 'which is to acquire gold, and to swell themselves with riches in a very brief time and thus rise to high estate disproportionate to their merits' – are the words of these priest-authors of today, when they describe the present political and economic arrangements across most of the continent:

> Such wealth allowed for the establishment of vast military, administrative and ecclesiastical bureaucracy, which came to control every detail of social life . . . they established an appropriate socio-economic and political system based on large land holdings and servility to foreign capital, and promoted cultural creativity merely as a local embodiment of foreign cultural traditions.

Thus, *The Voice of the Victims* is a deeply moving expression of the pain that came with Columbus in 1492 and has stayed permanently with the massive extending of his lucrative enterprise through history, and is a powerful repudiation of any celebratory response to 1992.

That the same publisher should produce, simultaneously, two books so implacably different about the same subject as Thomas's *Christopher Columbus* and Carpentier's *The Harp and the Shadow*, is perhaps indicative of the way in which contemporary commercial enterprises will treat the historical divide surrounding the navigator. As in the vision of Columbus, the 'divine metal' promises to shine for them, too, in 1992. Certainly, David A. Thomas's *Christopher Columbus: master of the Atlantic* [8] is in the celebratory vein, advertised as 'a lavishly illustrated, comprehensive and straightforward account of the great man and his achievements to complement the quincentennial celebrations of his discovery of the New World' – a sort of souvenir brochure to 1992 that is also something of a praise-song to the 'great discoverer', and typical of the kind of historical propaganda-piece that can be expected to set the laudatory tone for the quincentenary.

Thomas is not an original researcher, and quite openly admits that he has scoured the research of others. But he is undoubtedly an effective keeper and repeater of the myth, and combines this with a verve for topicalising history in crude and simplistic ways. Queen Isabella, requestor and protector of the Inquisition and directly responsible for the torture, death and pillaging of thousands of Spanish Jews, is considered as an 'enlightened monarch' who 'brought to her reign a Thatcher-like single-minded reforming zeal'. As for the people who Columbus met in the Caribbean, they were 'primitive natives', cannibals who 'ate anyone they managed to capture . . . As if in a butcher's shop, large cuts and joints from human bodies hung from huts', with those confined 'fattened like capons ready for the eating'. Thomas then adds a sick anecdote worthy of twentieth-century tabloid journalism: 'the natives were made violently sick after eating a friar, which thereafter gave a measure of protection for anyone wearing ecclesiastical clothes'. This is a marker for what threatens to pass as history and objective fact during the quincentenary.

Fortunate, then, that from the same publisher comes Alejo Carpentier's truly heretic novel of 1978 in its first translation from the Spanish: *The Harp and the Shadow*[9] – a genuine discovery for the English language in 1992. Nothing could be a more effective printed rejoinder to the previous volume under review than this novel by the great Cuban innovator of words and the historical imagination, who must have understood, over a decade before, what would need to be confronted and rebutted in 1992.

It is the mid-1880s. As the 'plagues' of socialism and communism and other radical ideas and 'dangerous Utopian visions' sweep across Europe, challenging Christian and conservative shibboleths, Pope Pius IX seeks an ideological antidote. As the 400th anniversary of Columbus's Caribbean landfall approaches, he thinks he has found what he needs in a scheme to beatify and eventually canonise the 'discoverer' himself – a figure of 'planetary wingspan' worthy of a prominent place in ' the litany of saints'. Accomplishing this, declares the pontiff, will counteract this 'dangerous passion of thinking' that is undermining the influence of his Church. This bold conception and its eventual failure comprise the first and last sections of the novel. The middle part is the story of Columbus's life, meditated by himself, as he lies dying and waiting for his confessor, dressed in a Franciscan habit in a 'sad Valladolid dusk'.

This most relentless and remorseful narrative is the 'Discoverer-discovered, uncovered', revealing to his own self-tortured soul the sordid chase for wealth and profit that was his life. It is Columbus unlearning himself. As he re-lives his career and travels, he begins to bask again in the 'glory I would achieve as the discoverer', as well as remembering the life of lies, masks and images of himself as he who 'defied the rages of nature and man' – the Herculean figure and 'magnifier' of the world who managed the 'most fabulous undertaking ever made'. Yet also looming into his consciousness are the deceptions and intrigues by which he lived as history's great charlatan, his lying and dissembling and all for 'gold, gold dust, gold bars, gold treasure chests, gold casks: the sweet music of gold coins clattering, spilling onto the banker's table: celestial music'. And with gold and the monstrous system supported by it, also the human material, the 'shit-assed Indians' that he enslaved and massacred in his attempts to 'substitute the flesh of the Indies for the gold of the Indies' – a labour value even greater than the obsessional gold, the 'irreplaceable energy of human flesh'. And we are back to, and forward to, the reality of 1992 in the slums of São Paulo and Lima, the canefields of the Dominican Republic, the tin mines of Bolivia or the banana lands of Honduras and Guatemala.

The Harp and the Shadow, although it spans the world and tells much of its story from Europe, could only have been made through the genius of a Caribbean writer, a novelist from the heart of the arc of islands that Columbus and his successors tore into and despoiled. Its publication is a rare triumph of the quincentenary and comes from a liberated mind in a liberated but isolated land, that has set aside the legacy of Columbus but which, in 1992, stands besieged and vulnerable, facing the hatred and weapons of the new imperialism of the America to the north.

Books reviewed

1   John Dyson and Peter Christopher, *Columbus: for gold, God and glory* (London, Hodder and Stoughton, 1991). 228pp., £19.95.

2   Homero Aridjis, *1492: the life and times of Juan Cabezon* (London, Andre Deutsch, 1991). 368pp., £14.99.

3   Hans Koning, *Columbus: his enterprise* (London, Latin America Bureau, 1991). 137pp., £4.99.

4   Felipe Fernandez-Armesto, *Columbus* (Oxford, Oxford University Press, 1991). 246pp., £16.95.

5   Kirkpatrick Sale, *The Conquest of Paradise: Christopher Columbus and the Columbian legacy* (London, Hodder and Stoughton, 1990). 384pp., £17.95.

6   Duncan Green, *Faces of Latin America* (London, Latin America Bureau, 1991). 200pp., £8.99.

7   Leonardo Boff and Virgil Elizondo (eds), *The Voice of the Victims, 1492-1992* (London, Concilium /SCM Press, 1990). 160pp., £8.95.

8   David A. Thomas, *Christopher Columbus: master of the Atlantic* (London, Andre Deutsch, 1991). 218pp., £14.99.

9   Alejo Carpentier, *The Harp and the Shadow* (London, Andre Deutsch, 1992). 159pp., £6.99.

BARBARA RANSBY

Columbus and the making of historical myth

As the world approaches the quincentennial commemoration of Christopher Columbus's accidental 'discovery' of America, we are reminded that history is, in large part, a battleground upon which scholars and activists fight to define the lens through which we will view the past. There is also a struggle to define which historical actors will be immortalised as heroes and heroines and which events will be emblazoned into our collective memory as turning-points and historical landmarks. How the story of Christopher Columbus should be told is at the centre of one such intellectual battle. The manufactured, but widely accepted, myth of Columbus as the brave and noble visionary who set sail on an unknown course and discovered a whole new world belies the real legacy of Columbus: a bloody legacy of rape, pillage and plunder. But, it is a myth which is quite consistent with how most of US history is recounted by mainstream historians – as great deeds by great white men which resulted in great things for all humankind. More specifically, it is a myth which celebrates imperial conquest, male supremacy and the triumph of military might as necessary components of progress and civilisation.

An examination of the Columbus myth illustrates how elites are able to justify their exploits under the guise of 'necessary evil'. Moreover, a survey of the treatment of Columbus in North American children's textbooks is a further indication of exactly how historical myths are made, and when and where the seeds of the dominant

Barbara Ransby is an African-American historian, activist and freelance journalist, and is co-founder of the Ella Baker-Nelson Mandela Center at the University of Michigan.

Race & Class, 33, 3 (1992)

culture are planted. To assess how most Americans are introduced to the story of Columbus in grade school, I examined thirty social studies textbooks published between 1966 and 1990 by major US publishers. Many of the newer texts are currently used in public schools throughout the US, the rest were the intellectual baby food of the current generation of college students.

In the overwhelming majority of writings about Columbus, particularly in children's books, there is a simplistic celebration of Columbus as a 'great discoverer [whose] courage opened a new world to Europeans', with little or no critical commentary.[1] In the majority of more 'enlightened' texts, however, there is an uncomfortable reconciliation of Columbus, the avaricious, slave-trading pirate, with Columbus, the brave and venturesome Italian mariner who paved the way for the expansion of western civilisation. Implicitly, of course, a new way could not be paved without the removal of obtrusive roadblocks to progress. Those roadblocks included millions of indigenous people who had lived on the lands Columbus supposedly discovered some 25,000 years before his expedition arrived. They were people who had names, cultures, belief systems and a history. They lived in harmony with an entire eco-system which was harshly disrupted with the arrival of European invaders in the 1490s. But elementary schoolchildren are told very little about the Taino and Carib peoples, and even less about the bloody conquest of their civilisations by the European colonisers we now celebrate as national icons. It is a conflict with which mainstream historians are quite uneasy because it does not fit neatly into the panoramic sweep of progress which is how many of them opt to characterise North American history. Many of these writers are much more comfortable quoting selectively from Columbus's journal about how he admired the gentleness and generosity of the 'Indians', carefully omitting his conclusion that their kind and calm demeanour would make them easier to exploit and enslave.

Most children's textbooks also fail to mention that Columbus actually introduced the slave trade to the Americas. When he was unsuccessful in his desperate search for gold and other natural riches in the islands of the Caribbean, he began sending human cargo back to Spain instead. Hundreds of Taino and Carib Indians were torn from their homes and families and shipped to Europe to be sold as servants and slaves in the decades after Columbus's arrival. Social studies texts, for the most part, omit, gloss over or reconstruct this ignominious episode in early American history. One text euphemistically describes the six Tainos Columbus forcibly took back to Spain on his first return trip as his 'guests'.[2] Another text, which admits that the colonisers killed thousands of Indians, still describes the system of coerced labour set up by Columbus in the following terms: 'Columbus tried to make use of the Indians by requiring them to bring him gold and to work for his colonies.'[3] This passage seems to suggest that the native people were idle and unproductive before Columbus's arrival and required his assistance in finding 'useful' and productive work.

Ultimately, the popular myths surrounding Columbus serve as subtle, and sometimes not so subtle, justifications for both male supremacy and white supremacy. Schoolchildren are taught, through omissions, euphemisms and outright distortions, that conquest is a heroic, masculine enterprise worthy of emulation, and that, when the casualties of such conquests are uncivilised people of colour, they are expendable. Three hundred and fifty years after Columbus's initial invasion of the Caribbean, US president Andrew Jackson, himself engaged in a campaign to finish off the process of Native American genocide begun by Columbus, summed up the necessity of the early conquest in these words: 'What good man would prefer a country covered with forests and ranged by a few thousand savages to our extensive republic, studded with cities, towns, and prosperous farms . . . filled with the blessings of liberty, civilisation, and religion?'[4] According to historian Ron Takaki, during the nineteenth century, the ruling elite of the US concluded that 'white violence was a necessary partial evil for the realisation of a general good – the extension of white civilisation and the transformation of the wilderness into an agrarian society'.[5]

Most Americans know, in some vague sense, the grim fate that befell the native populations of the Caribbean islands after Columbus's advent. Within fifty years of the arrival of the European invaders, a population of over 300,000 native people was wholly decimated, with not one member surviving by 1540.[6] This was due in part to disease and displacement, but much of it was due to outright brutality and savagery on the part of the invaders, who waged genocidal wars against those they perceived as obstructions to progress. Women were raped, the environment was ravaged and, eventually, most of what had existed before was destroyed. The land was cleared for the building of a new world. Columbus initially described the so-called Indians he met as 'gentle souls', but when they refused to acquiesce passively to his plans for their subjugation, he was relentless in his brutality against them. Columbus biographer Kirkpatrick Sale describes a scene near the colony of Isabela in 1495:

> to subdue the recalcitrant natives and tame the countryside . . . the soldiers mowed down dozens with point blank volleys, loosed the dogs to rip open limbs and bellies, chased fleeing Indians into the bush to skewer them on sword and pike, and 'with God's aid soon gained a complete victory, killing many Indians and capturing others who were also killed'. Of the valley that was Paradise they made a desert, and called it peace.[7]

Moreover, what happened in the Caribbean islands in the 1490s and early 1500s was only a dress rehearsal for what was to transpire on the North American mainland some 300 years later.

Even though most Americans do not know, or choose not to know, all the gory details of the Columbian conquest, there is a general awareness among most that genocide did occur and that a people was annihilated. Authors of children's texts about Columbus, as hard as they try to evade the brual truth, are often forced to admit that 'the Indians were treated unfairly', and 'many Indians died'. Yet, both in popular myth and in written texts, authors have attempted to reconcile the good and the bad in the Columbian legacy, minimising the latter and highlighting the former. 'He had his faults, but . . .' is the sentiment echoed throughout many of the writings about him.

The reticence of scholars to dethrone Columbus, despite the admitted atrocities he committed, is reflected in the following quote by the Columbian researcher and Pulitzer prize winner, John Noble Wilford:

> We do know he was an inept governor of the Spanish settlements in the Caribbean and had a bloodied hand in the brutalisation of the native people and in the start of the slave trade. But we are left wondering if he is to be admired and praised, condemned – or perhaps pitied as a tragic figure.[8]

Despite his admission that Columbus murdered and enslaved Indian people, Wilford is still uncertain whether such behaviour really warrants condemnation. He speculates that perhaps the significance of such actions is outweighed by Columbus's own personal tragedies. Similarly, other texts mention Columbus's reprehensible deeds, but describe them in such dispassionate terms that they seem almost benign. One 1990 textbook casually refers to the genocidal conquest of the native peoples in this way: 'Though they had a keen interest in the peoples of the Caribbean, Columbus and his crews were never able to live peacefully among them.'[9] The author seems perplexed by the fact that the enslavement of native people and the theft of their land was any cause for tension between them and the European invaders. He is also reluctant to assign blame for the mysterious conflict, as indicated by his ambiguous and neutral choice of words. What such erroneous formulations effectively do is reduce the crimes against native people to footnotes in a larger, implicitly more important, text. The main story is about the greatness of western civilisation, the march of progress, the triumph of civilisation over savagery, Christianity over heathenism, and the imposition of order upon the chaos of the wilderness. This is a fundamentally racist formulation, consistent with the ways in which the subjugation and massacre of people of colour have been rationalised both by scholars and by ruling elites for generations. In fact, the rationalisation offered by the apologists for Native American genocide sounds frighteningly similar to the justification for the recent Gulf war. The murder of thousands of Iraqi civilians was described as an unfortunate but necessary action, taken in order to abate the greater evil of unchecked barbarism.

While the Columbian myth is both an American and a European one, it has a special significance in the context of US history and folklore. Even though Columbus was a European, and his first voyage predated the American revolution by nearly 300 years, he is revered by many as the first American hero. The nation's capital is named in his honour, as are several US cities, streets, parks and schools, including one of the country's oldest and most prestigious universities. His birthday is a federal holiday and the US government intends to spend millions of dollars in 1992 to commemorate the quincentenary of his initial transatlantic voyage. The legacy of Columbus has become an integral part of the annals of North American history because it fits so neatly into a larger scenario which celebrates the so-called pioneer spirit as that which has propelled the US to its current greatness. And, after all, Columbus was the first pioneer, followed by the Pilgrims, the cowboys, and US troops guarding the new frontiers of democracy around the globe today. Columbus was one among many great white explorers who courageously ventured into the darkness of the unknown, only to find a wilderness crying out to be tamed. The wilderness included both the land and its people. When the newly formed US began the process of constructing a national identity and culture, the memory of Christopher Columbus was resurrected as a symbol of the virtues of rugged individualism, stoic determination and a ruthless pioneer spirit which the young republic sought to instil in its citizens. It is no coincidence then that in 1692, the bicentennial of Columbus's fateful voyage, there were no great celebrations in the American colonies. But 100 years later, in the immediate wake of the American revolution, Columbus was lauded in commemorative festivities throughout the newly independent nation.[10]

It is also significant, and not at all surprising, that the blatantly racist and sexist nature of the Columbian conquest has in no way diminished the great discoverer's status as an enduring and celebrated American hero. While most children's books essentially ignore the issue of gender and minimise the issue of race in re-telling the story of Columbus, both race and sex are integral features of the conquest of the Caribbean islands. The racist nature of the conquest is readily apparent. Repeatedly, in the descriptions of the world Columbus 'discovered', the native population is referred to as part of the natural landscape, nearly indistinguishable from the other wild creatures who inhabited the islands. The following passage is typical: '[Columbus] returned to Spain taking with him a few of the curious copper-skinned natives, some birds, and some fish which he found'.[11]. No distinction is made by this writer between Columbus's human and non-human souvenirs. Children reading such a passage could easily be left with the impression that the significance of those copper-skinned human beings was no greater than that of the captured fish or birds.

Initially, the native people were described by Columbus as generous and docile creatures. Later, when they got a taste of what their European visitors had in store for them and began to resist colonisation and 'progress', Columbus increasingly characterised them as 'cannibalistic savages' who had to be beaten into submission or extinction.[12] Columbus's animosity towards the native people was not the result of some innate aversion to people of colour or any xenophobic aversion to difference, as indicated by his initially favourable description of them. Rather, deeming them 'racially', socially and culturally inferior served as a convenient rationale for confiscating their land, usurping their labour and, eventually, annihilating them as a people. In fact, it was not their dark skin which Columbus alleged was an indicator of their inferiority, but their culture, their way of life and that fact that they did not embrace Christianity. After all, the Moors and Jews had just been expelled from Spain for the same reasons by Columbus's benefactor, Queen Isabella. So, as early as the fifteenth century, the notion of an inferior 'breed' of men and women served as reason for their exploitation and subjugation.

Columbus's legacy is not only that of racism and imperialism, but of sexual conquest as well. According to Kirkpatrick Sale, 'the women of America were as much a part of the bounty due the conquering Europeans as the other resources in which it luxuriated'.[13] Native American women, like their African and African-American counterparts centuries later, were victims of sexual terrorism as a part of the larger scenario of conquest and colonisation. An Italian sailor, who was a part of Columbus's entourage when he invaded Santa Cruz island, described in his journal a scene that was probably typical:

> I captured a very beautiful Carib woman whom the Lord Admiral [Columbus] gave me, and with whom, having taken her into my cabin, she being naked according to their custom, I conceived desire to take pleasure [rape her]. I wanted to put my desire into execution but she did not want it and treated me with her finger nails in such a manner that I wished I had never begun . . . I took a rope and thrashed her well, for which she raised such unheard of screams that you would not have believed your ears.[14]

The rape of Indian women was not uncommon, but seems to have been systematic and routine. Another member of Columbus's crew described the situation in the colony of La Navidad in 1493: 'Bad feelings arose and broke out into warfare because of the licentious conduct of our men towards the Indian women.'[15]

Moreover, the story of Columbus's voyage is, above all, characterised as an adventure story in which men, more specifically European men, are the principal, if not the sole, cognisant actors. It is recounted as a romantic tale of fearless seamen who set out to explore the far reaches of the earth, only to stumble upon a treasure greater than they could have imagined, a new world. It is couched as a distinctly male adventure, a biased but favourable characterisation which ignores and minimises the very real experiences of the native women who were some of the chief victims of the conquest and colonisation.

Schoolchildren in the US are encouraged to view Columbus as a great hero, the Admiral of the Ocean Sea. Most of them learn the familiar rhyme: 'In 1492, Columbus sailed the ocean blue', which firmly implants the legendary figure in their memories. They are even encouraged to learn from, and emulate, his example. One popular text urges teachers to highlight Columbus's virtues so that children see the benefits of patience and courage. And, since most public schools in western nations socialise children not to be critical thinkers, but to be good citizens, hard workers and, if need be, loyal soldiers, the myth of Columbus serves those purposes well. Moreover, openly to acknowledge the brutal and unsavoury origins of European influence in the western hemisphere would mean confronting the bloody traditions spawned from those beginnings. Therefore, Columbus's image has been scrubbed clean and sanitised by many generations of American historians so that he can now be offered up as a sterling example of the glorious era of discovery. His weaknesses, mistakes and horrid transgressions are all excused in the name of progress. The construction of the heroic myth and legend surrounding Columbus also belies the notion that the writing of history is an objective enterprise. And it further underscores the contention that history is ultimately written by the victors, and by those with the power and resources to publish, distribute and thus validate the version of history which best serves the interests of the status quo.

So, in 1992, it is a quite ignoble band of pioneers, with Columbus at the helm, that Americans will celebrate so lavishly on the occasion of the quincentenary. There will be travelling museum exhibitions, elaborate parades and commemorative ceremonies. In Puerto Rico, there will be a flotilla of ships bearing the names of the original three ships sailed by Columbus in 1492 and a re-enactment of the invasion, euphemistically referred to as the landing. And the government of the Dominican Republic is organising an 'archaeological reconstruction' of one of Columbus's unsuccessful Caribbean colonies established in 1494.[16] But, just as native people fought to defend their culture and their lives against imperialist hegemony five centuries ago, today progressive historians, activists and the political descendants of those first American freedom-fighters are struggling to resist yet another insult upon the memory of those who died.

American Indian Movement leader Russel Means once compared the legacy of Columbus to the legacy of Hitler. Native Americans and their allies throughout the Americas are determined that such a legacy not be celebrated without visible, vocal and militant opposition. Counter-demonstrations, days of mourning for the victims of genocide and de-commemoration ceremonies are planned throughout the year by groups ranging from the Women of All Red Nations to a multicultural group of educator-activists, called REPOhistory. An intercontinental run for peace and dignity is also planned which will include participants from north, central and south America. One set of runners will begin in Argentina, another in Alaska and the tour will culminate in a ceremony and rally in Mexico City. The general purpose is to link the native communities throughout the hemisphere and to celebrate a common history of resistance and survival – in spite of Columbus. These are but a few of the many efforts underway to reclaim, inch by inch, the confiscated territory which is our history.

References

1   Allen Y. King, I. Dennis and F. Potter, *The United States and the Other Americas* (New York, 1978), p.47. Other sources used for this article include R.C. Brown and H.J. Bass, *One Flag, One Nation* (Morristown, NJ., 1985); Christopher Columbus, *Journal of First Voyage* (New York, 1924); D.T. Gerace (ed), *Columbus and His World: proceedings of the first San Salvador conference* (Ft. Lauderdale, Fl., 1987); H.F. Graff, *America: the glorious republic* (Boston, 1986); H.F. Graff and P. Bohannan, *The Call of Freedom: the grand experiment* (New York, 1978); L.S. Kenworthy, *One Nation: the United States* (Lexington, 1972); S.E. Morison, *Admiral of the Sea* (Boston, 1942); P.E. Taviani, *Christopher Columbus: the grand design* (London, 1985).
2   George Shaftel, *Decisions in United States History* (Lexington, Mass., 1972), p. 19.
3   D. Buggey et al, *America, America* (Glenview, Il., 1977), p. 65.
4   Quoted in Ronald T. Takaki, *Iron Cages: race and culture in nineteenth century America* (Seattle, 1979), p. 103.
5   Ibid.
6   Buggey, op. cit., p. 65.
7   Kirkpatrick Sale, *The Conquest of Paradise: Christopher Columbus and the Columbian legacy* (New York, 1990), p. 154.
8   J.N. Wilford, 'Discovering Columbus', in *New York Times Magazine* (11 August, 1991).
9   Clarence L. Ver Steeg, *The American Spirit: a history of the American people* (Englewood, NJ., 1990), p. 262.
10 Wilford, op. cit.
11 Heller and Potter, *One Nation Indivisible* (Columbus, Ohio, 1966), p.8.
12 G. Shaftel, *Decisions in United States History* (Lexington, Mass., 1972).
13 Sale, op. cit., p. 141.
14 Ibid., p. 140.
15 Ibid., p. 139.
16 Ibid. p. 143.

The aftermath

Spain: the Day of the Race

In 1898, as a result of its disastrous war with the US, Spain was forced to relinquish possession of Cuba, the Philippines and Puerto Rico, the last remaining territories in the empire established nearly four centuries before in the wake of the *Reconquista* and the invasion of the Americas. Apart from a few enclaves in North Africa, which were to be the cause of further humiliations in the years to come, Spain had effectively ceased to be an imperial power. Despite the speed with which the final collapse occurred, however, the end of empire was in fact the logical outcome of a long-term process of internal disintegration that had been in progress since about the middle of the seventeenth century. Ironically, the same forces which had shaped Spain's rapid ascent to imperial greatness at the beginning of the sixteenth century were, in many ways, responsible for the country's subsequent decline. The dizzying successes achieved by Spanish feats of arms during the aggressive expansion of Castille and Aragon consolidated a social structure that was ill-equipped, in the long term, to administer the vast empire that had come under its control. Among its elements were an aristocratic military caste that glorified warfare and spurned trade and commerce; a fanatical and reactionary clergy, hostile to any new ideas that threatened its monolithic ideological grip on Spanish society, and a succession of absolutist rulers who drained the wealth and resources of the empire in ruinous religious wars.

As a result, while other countries in Europe were laying the economic foundations for the industrial revolution through the establishment of a mercantile economy, Spain lagged behind the economic and political developments taking place beyond the Pyrenees, and its extensive empire concealed the stagnation that was taking place in the metropolis itself. Large-scale emigration to the New World and the expulsion of the Jewish and Arab populations further compounded the country's economic decay. Even in 1640 the sickness was already obvious to many, and the solution to Spain's problems was described to the King's minister Olivares by the rebellious Catalans as 'repopulate the country, cultivate our fields, fortify our cities, open our ports to commerce and re-establish our factories . . . the treasure from America should be spent on this and not on senseless and disgraceful wars'.[1]

By the beginning of the twentieth century, therefore, the gulf between Spain and its northern neighbours had grown so wide that the country had become a political and economic anachronism in western Europe; an over-centralised state ruled by a corrupt and parasitic bureaucracy; an archaic landowning structure dominated by large estates, and a powerful Catholic Church that continued to fight the spread of secular ideas with the same virulent hostility that it had displayed towards the reformation during the sixteenth century. The loss of its overseas empire exacerbated the sense of national crisis, accelerating the process of social and political disintegration that was to explode into civil war. Separatism, the spread of liberal, socialist and anarchist ideas and the eruption of centuries-old class hatreds – all these forces combined to threaten the unity of the Spanish state and the reactionary social order that it supported. The result was the military uprising of 1936 against the Republican government, and the imposition of the Francoist dictatorship after three years of bloody civil war which left the country virtually in ruins. Although the disintegration of the Spanish state had been halted, as that state had been founded, by force, its isolation from the rest of Europe continued to undermine its economic recovery, and its social and political structures remained anachronistic in comparison with the rest of the continent.

All this helps to explain the obsession with modernisation, in all senses, that has been so evident in Spain during the democratic era. Today, on the eve of the millenium, a resurgent, self-confident Spain is preparing for the twenty-first century with an intensive programme of economic and political renovation under the leadership of the Spanish Socialist Workers Party (PSOE). Since coming to power, the PSOE has assumed the responsibility for remodelling Spanish society on liberal-capitalist lines with a single-minded enthusiasm that would certainly have surprised the party's more radical founders. The entry into the EC, the drastic industrial restructuring of the early 1980s and Spain's integration into NATO are all evidence of the ruling party's determination to break the country's historical isolation from the rest of Europe. Implicit in this project of modernisation is the notion of making Spain a great power again, both within Europe and beyond. The increasingly high-profile activity of Spanish diplomacy in the international arena, the hostility to Cuba, and the PSOE's eager participation in the destruction of Iraq are part of this process, as Spain seeks to carve a niche for itself in the new world order.

*   *   *

In this context, the celebrations of 1992 assume an enormous symbolic importance for the architects of Spain's transformation, in which the commemoration of the transcendental events of 1492 have become an ideal opportunity to project Spain back onto the world stage in the twenty-first century. The World Fair in Seville, the Olympic games in Barcelona, the nomination of Madrid as the cultural capital of Europe are only the most prominent events designed to place Spain at the centre of international attention during 1992. Amid the gala celebrations, the VIP summits and the historical pageantry, a critical appraisal of Spanish history is not very high on the official agenda. In spite of the official quincentennial commission's invocation of 1992 as an occasion 'to stop and reflect on the past', there is very little evidence that such a process is taking place. Instead of reflecting on, or even recognising, the destructive and aggressive nature of the conquest, or the disastrous consequences of its imperialist venture on Spain itself, what is offered is a sanitised version of the past to suit the interests of the present holders of economic and political power on both sides of the Atlantic. In virtually all official speeches and writings on 1992, the genocide, slavery and violence which accompanied the dawn of the Spanish empire are either conspicuous by their absence, or couched in euphemisms and vague allusions. While the campaign against the celebrations has resulted in a moderation of the triumphal-ist tone of official speeches in recent months, it is clear that the negative consequences of 1492 will not be allowed to overshadow what the Mexican writer Carlos Fuentes, at a gala celebration in New York, recently called 'the greatness of the encounter between Spaniards and Americans'.

Purged of the greed, racism and fanaticism which inspired it, the Spanish conquest of Latin America is presented as an entirely positive and even benevolent process, in which Columbus's 'discovery' of the New World becomes a metaphor for the triumph of progress and modernity, and the celebration of his achievements becomes a celebration of the Spanish contribution to European civilisation and a transatlantic Ibero-american community with a 'common language and culture'.

The chauvinistic interpretation of Columbus as a uniquely Spanish hero is nothing new. During the Franco dictatorship, the discovery of America on 12 October 1492 was commemorated in an annual holiday called the 'Day of the Race'. In the democratic era, the name of the holiday has been changed to the 'Day of *Hispanidad*', but its purpose remains the same – to glorify a fundamentally Castilian culture that was imposed by force on both the Iberian peninsula and Latin America itself. The concept of a homogenous Hispanic civilisation not only excludes the indigenous peoples of Latin America who do not share the 'common language and culture', it also obscures the fact that Spain has never been a homogenous nation itself, but rather a loose conglomeration of entirely distinct languages and cultures grouped together under the military and political domination of Castille.[2] For the Catalan and Basque nationalists, for example, who suffered the suppression of their language and culture for centuries, the concept of a transcendent '*Hispanidad*' is as meaningless and devoid of historical accuracy as it is for the descendents of the Mayans or the Incas. As Ronald Fraser[3] has pointed out, the military uprising of 1936 was prompted as much by the army's hostility to the separatist aspirations of the Basque country and Catalonia as it was by the fear of social revolution, and the ruthless imposition of *Hispanidad* on these rebellious regions was one of the consequences of the republican defeat. Today, the national holiday continues, and, in 1990, was enthusiastically celebrated by over 400 skinheads, members of far-Right and fascist groups, who went on a violent rampage through the centre of Barcelona to express their adherence to Spanish culture and civilisation.

Despite its contradictions, however, the projection of a shared Hispanic civilisation on both sides of the Atlantic remains one of the dominant themes in the 1992 celebrations. Entirely forgetting the original purpose of the conquest, the exploitative nature of the relationship between Spain and its conquered territories, and the long and often brutal struggle of these same colonies to free themselves from Spanish domination during the last century, official statements are fond of referring to the '500-year dialogue' between 'two peoples', which began with Columbus's visionary expedition beyond the frontiers of the known world. The silver mines of Potosi, where thousands of Indian slaves were worked to death in subhuman conditions; the extermination of the indigenous population of Hispaniola following Columbus's arrival, or the ferocious repression of the Cuban rebellion at the end of the last century – all these events are confined to historical oblivion or dismissed as 'sterile polemics' by the organisers of the quincentennial. 'Any debate is good for Spain', said the Spanish embassy's official consultant on the quincentennial in Washington recently, 'because it serves to clarify and demonstrate the achievements of the Spanish legacy and also serves to eliminate the "black legend" that has surrounded the role of Spain in America for 500 years'.

The elimination of that 'black legend' is clearly one of the main tasks of the 1992 extravaganza. In recent years, Spain has sought to strengthen cultural, political and economic links with its 'brother countries' in Latin America in order to continue what King Juan Carlos described as 'the great work carried out in 500 years'. The re-invention of the past occurs at a time when Spanish capital, increasingly squeezed out of the domestic economy, and anxious about its ability to compete in the new united Europe, has begun to look for new areas of investment in its former colonies. The moves towards political and economic integration in the southern cone countries, and the wave of IMF-directed privatisations taking place across the continent, have prompted an increase in foreign investment in Latin America which Spain is in a good position to take advantage of.[4] In Argentina, for example, where the drastic economic reforms implemented by Carlos Menem have resulted in thousands of public-sector workers losing their jobs, Spanish public corporations have been particularly active, buying large shares in the newly-privatised state companies such as the national airlines and the Buenos Aires electricity service. Similar investments have been made in Chile and Uruguay and other projects are being planned for the future, as some economic experts predict an 'investment fever' in those countries where the IMF reforms have gone furthest. With the average per capita income in Latin America lower than it was ten years ago, and many countries threatened by a cholera epidemic due to the absence of basic, primary health care facilities, the parcelling out of key sections of the national economy to foreign companies seems to be a dubious way of achieving the long-term economic development which is one of the stated goals of the quincentennial commission. On the contrary, the new economic links being forged between the mother country and the right-wing democracies in Latin America could more accurately be described as a perpetuation of the underdevelopment which is also part of the legacy of 'the meeting between two worlds'.

*   *   *

The enormous official commitment to the quincentennial, and the prestigious names on both sides of the Atlantic who have lent their support to it, have naturally tended to marginalise the critical voices that have been raised against the proceedings from indigenous groups and solidarity activists. While Spanish public opinion has remained largely indifferent to the historical debate, a number of events are being planned over the coming twelve months in order to raise public consciousness about the issues involved and present an alternative interpretation of the past to the official version. In June 1992, the Conference of Stateless Peoples will be held in Barcelona in the same month as the Olympic games, with representatives from indigenous groups from all over the world. The following month, an alternative Latin American summit is planned to coincide with the Ibero-american summit conference in Madrid. The climax of the national campaign against the 1992 celebrations will take place on 12 October, the day of *Hispanidad*, when the first monument to the victims of Spanish colonialism will be publicly unveiled in the town of Puerto Real, near Cadiz. The monument has been commissioned from the Latin American sculptor Oswaldo Guayasamin, and its inauguration will be attended by representatives from national and international organisations in Europe and Latin America that have participated in the campaign.

Apart from these actions, local campaigners across Spain have concentrated their efforts on consciousness-raising and the production of educational materials for Spanish schools. In a country where the conquest of Latin America is still described in many textbooks as 'the invasion of the barbarian peoples', and where historical truth has too often been obscured by the chauvinist myths of *Hispanidad*, the work being carried out by dissident anthropologists and academics associated with the campaign, such as Jesus Contreras,[5] provides one of the few public examples of genuine reflection on the past to be found amid the general atmosphere of triumphalism and smug complacency exuding from official circles and the mass media. Between the active censorship of the past practised by the Franco dictatorship and the historical revisionism implicit in the 1992 celebrations, there is little difference in substance – only in style. Whereas Franco once called on the spirit of Isabella the Catholic and the *Reconquista* to justify his violent crusade on behalf of a reactionary social order, the media barons, technocrats and bankers who rule the new, democratic Spain have interpreted the triumph of Castille as the dawn of progress. 'The journey of Columbus', said Jesus de Polanco, the president of *El Pais*, at a recent VIP dinner in New York, 'was the first great adventure in the era of communications, in which the mass media, with the diffusion of knowledge, contributed to the understanding of peoples and the progress of humanity'.

Such vacuous pronouncements are indicative of the depths of the 'reflection' which the 1992 extravaganza is intended to provoke. At times, the chauvinistic glorification of all things Spanish and the wilful historical amnesia that has accompanied it border on the idiotic, such as the incredible response of the government and mass media to the staging of the Middle East conference in Madrid. The PSOE's reward for its enthusiastic participation in the destruction of Iraq was hailed almost universally as yet another triumph for Spanish culture, prompting a series of official statements and articles on Spain's historical role as the meeting place of Judaism, Islam and Christianity. That both the Jewish and Arab civilisations in Spain were destroyed by the same racist, fundamentalist Catholic order whose rise to power is being celebrated in 1992, or that Spain has some of the toughest immigration laws in Europe, specifically directed against poor migrants from North Africa, did nothing to detract from the cosy image of Spanish tolerance which made Madrid 'the city of peace'.

None of this is likely to get any better over the next twelve months. As the Spain of fast money, conspicuous consumption and routine corruption prepares to pay homage to the Holy Empire of the Catholic Monarchs, the gushing prose and the chauvinistic pronouncements are certain to increase in volume, their dishonesty matched only by their banality. At the same time, the 'meeting place of three civilisations' continues to fulfil its new historical role as the geographical frontier against what Jean Marie Le Pen recently called 'the invasion of Arab immigrants from North Africa' – with the deportation of 'undesirables' facilitated by the recent changes in the immigration laws. Nor are African and Arab migrants likely to be the only victims. The mass deportation of a group of Peruvians from Barcelona during the summer, and the violent police attack on a demonstration by Quechua Indians in Seville, provide small indications that the official concept of an Ibero-american community has its limitations. The upsurge in popular racism all over the continent has also made itself apparent in Spain, where there has been a sharp increase in fascist activity, as well as a number of violent attacks and demonstrations against the gypsy population. In October 1991, a new and dangerous phenomenon made its appearance in Spanish cities for the first time – spontaneous vigilante patrols engaging in violent attacks on suspected drug addicts and drug dealers. In some cities the brutal witch-hunt of drug addicts took on an openly racist hue, with public demonstrations against the planned construction of cheap housing for the gypsy population and attacks on gypsy settlements. In the town of La Mancha, angry mothers demonstrated against the introduction of gypsy children into a public school, gathering outside the main entrance to scream abuse as the children came to school in the morning.

All this is also part of the millenial celebrations. At the same time as the dominant, mercantile industrial civilisation prepares to display its technological achievements in Seville, the majority of the world's population remains excluded from 500 years of progress and the bureaucrats of the new united Europe are erecting new barriers to prevent an 'invasion' from the poor and dispossessed. At the end of the twentieth century, Spain once again finds itself on the frontier, waiting for the barbarians, and prepares to take its place in the new world order with a celebration of its contribution to the old.

Barcelona   MATTHEW CARR

References

1   Gerald Brenan, *The Spanish Labyrinth* (Cambridge, 1960).
2   Americo Castro, *Sombre el nombre y el quien de los Espanoles* (Sarpe, 1985).
3   Ronald Fraser, *Blood of Spain* (Harmondsworth, 1981).
4   See *America 92: Revista del Quinto Centenario* (September 1991).
5   Jesus Contreras (compiler), *Identidad etnica y movimientos indios* (Madrid, Ed. Revolucion, 1988).

The reality of Latin America*

Why so much deliberation about the identity of our continent?
I am amazed when I perceive how fascinated the developed
countries of the west are by the study and discussion of this theme,
especially since it is they who are the cause of so much humiliation, by
word and deed, to the debtor countries of the so-called Third World. I
ask myself: do they feel remorse because they don't really know us? Is
it because we are special or undefinable? Is it because Latin America
is a continent still searching for its true identity?

Europe is a reality fed by a long tradition through which its people
recognise each other, reinforce each other and to a great extent
sustain each other. The US, with which it shares a common profile, is
an extension of the same process.

Europeans have forgotten their finest values. Although they retain
their cultural heritage, they prefer, for the most part, the expensive
and dehumanising trinkets of consumerist society. I invite you to step
out of your gloom, citizens of the old continent: you have conquered
everything, and all that you have gained is individual isolation. Now it
is your turn to discover and regain for yourselves a sense of community
with all humankind.

For its part, Latin America has never ceased welcoming its own
identity with open arms. It stands half way, as it were, between
Europe and its indigenous and African past. Its identity is its
diversity.

No-one can deny that our continent with its mixture of races is an
extension of western culture, and, to a lesser extent, of the African
and Oriental. We are as much the inheritors of Iberian civilisation as
any inhabitant of Salamanca or Vallodolid. They, too, were suckled
on English, French and Italian culture, just to mention the most
influential. We are a synthesis of Spanish, indigenous and African, not
forgetting Portuguese, English, French and Dutch. We have been
pieced together out of fragments from almost all the world, a sort of
jigsaw puzzle of world culture. The mystery of this interwoven fabric
explains our originality.

*   *   *

Since Columbus's mistaken but unambiguous adventure, America has

* Shortened version of a lecture by Tomàs Borge, delivered in Spain, summer 1990.
First published in *1992 and the New World – 500 years of resistance,* journal of the
Leicester-Masaya Link Group (1991).

been the promised land. We have for centuries been the land where blood is mingled into rare quintessences, despite the fact that, from the first moment of conquest, it was the invader's intention to impose his identity upon us.

From that time on, to mitigate their inherited pangs of remorse, we have had to be what Europeans wanted us to be. Europeans in their arrogance are irritated when we react with dignity. And when reality in all its variety does not coincide with their illusions, they feel swindled. Frequently this results in withdrawal of financial aid. So, returning to our theme: to what extent is Latin America a myth, to what extent reality? Which is subordinate to which? Is the myth the source of the reality, or vice versa?

One way or another, our approach to these questions places us right in the middle of contemporary Latin American philosophy, also called for obvious reasons the philosophy of liberation. It is a philosophy which has developed its themes from the thoughts of many of the founders of modern Hispano-American culture. It is concerned with an integrative and kindly humanism, which considers the liberation of humanity as the basic objective of culture. Hegel stated that Europe was the mistress of history, the incarnation of pure spirit, since Europeans, and they only, had been capable of developing a form of consciousness which sustained their image of themselves. Ours was an unknown land, but it was here that liberty would be achieved. Inventors of utopias locate their scenarios in our continent. The libertarian and romantic thinkers of the nineteenth century dreamed of a corner of American soil in which to spin their fantasies.

Latin America does not make sense without its myths. They are a tempting vision for Europeans and a sop to the conscience of the coloniser and neo-coloniser. Latin American reality, however, is the flesh which surrounds the myths. Because of Europe's inability to realise its own era of liberation, European rationalists and humanists have transposed on to the recently discovered continent the myth of the Promised Land, the Golden Age, the Noble Savage. This mythical reality is what gave rise to the image of Latin America. Latin America, land of liberty and imagination, this is the great fundamental myth. The sources of American inventiveness are: exoticism, exuberance, rarity, virginity, the enormous extensiveness of our lands. It is these which engender the idea of liberty and convert the abstraction into reality.

Discovering the reality leads to an increase in wonder. Latin America is the place where the impossible is possible. Only here could a president weep when an ant was crushed, while rejoicing at the genocide of thousands of his compatriots. And why? Ants do not survive beyond death, whereas humans could die because their souls were immortal. Only in that part of the world could a dictator keep in the garden of his house, in two identical cages, panthers and political prisoners, for the personal enjoyment of his family. Our epic story and our unusual achievements contrast with these aberrations. Some of the finest utopias from that America which we refer to as 'ours' have been the Mexican, Cuban and Nicaraguan revolutions.

But once we have reached such a point, we have to ask: do myth and reality coincide in Latin America? Has the era of liberty, as Hegel wished it to be, really happened in our midst? Or does the myth function as an accursed mechanism to distort reality? Let us not forget that for us the concept of liberty has an all-encompassing dimension, since we identify it with life and hope. It is no accident that the poet Reuben Dario entitled the book he wrote in his maturity, *Songs of Life and Hope*. In those miraculous poems we come across questions about the destiny of our people and our race, about our national and continental identity, similar to the investigations of philosophers and political scientists. Dario foresaw the tough, tragic destiny of Latin America and the deadly arrogance of North American imperialism.

Our lands have been on offer to every humanist and libertarian experiment, to every utopia, starting with scholastic and Renaissance humanism. They were betrayed by conquest and colonialism, and now, having passed through independence liberalism and positivism during our republican period, marxism-leninism and liberation theology are the dominant themes. So far, with certain exceptions, these European ideologies have all been ethnocentric and exclusive. The results are patent. After an instant of momentum – frustration; after initial euphoria – abandonment; ideas dashed to fragments against the irritation of reality. Only marxism in its truly subversive form, stripped of all vestiges of stalinism, has to a great extent satisfied our expectations.

It may seem that our America has got used to this ebb and flow. We tend to take on board the most fashionable theory which comes to us from Europe or the US and apply it to our reality. We often do not apply wise and just doctrines. So it is amazing that so many thinkers and leaders should have studied and managed to put into practice, with the force of their own vision, the miracle of marxist theory. This confirms its universal character.

Instead of looking at ourselves, instead of analysing our own reality, our thinking, our myths, we are intent on testing to see if what we do is in accordance with European values. Just like nineteenth-century liberals, who totally denied colonial culture, we have in general tended to be text-book marxists, seeking to fit concepts derived from manuals into our disproportionate view of reality. No one discusses the real need for text-books, though we sometimes discuss their deficiencies. No one discusses how the effect of rituals and catechisms is to cause our thinking and our social action to fossilise. We rarely refer to the classics, to real life or to the imagination. We rarely allow ourselves an irreverent leap into creativity. There is no doubt that this is one of the fundamental characteristics of Latin American culture, the slavish adoption of new schemes and ideologies when we have not yet finished absorbing the previous ones. This is due amongst other things to our lack of any critical or philosophical tradition. Nor do we, as yet, have anything which could be called a theoretical system of our own, although it seems to me that a contemporary Europe has nothing similar to Che Guevara either. For Che is not only the moral and strategic archetype of guerrilla war. He is, above all, a person who critically assimilated marxist theory and experience, with his feet firmly on the ground.

Twenty years before perestroika, Che rebelled against a notion of socialism which, in the majority of Eastern European countries, put into practice the 'effacement of the individual on the altars of the state'. But, at the same time, he saw the pathway towards these reforms which were so urgently needed and he saw them in what he called real socialism. In my opinion, this is the core of his thinking. Che would remind those who proclaim market economics as the panacea which will save eastern Europe from its relative economic prostration that, as long as the market is the economic driving force in society, 'its effects will be felt in the organisation of production and, in the final analysis, in the consciousness of the people'. At the beginning of the 1960s, in his journeys through the socialist landscape, he warned that 'the temptation to follow the well-trodden tracks of material interest as an accelerator of development' was great:

> The illusion of developing a socialist project with the battered tools bequeathed to us by capitalism can lead us into a blind alley. On the way, many tracks criss-cross again and again and it is hard to know where you got lost. Meanwhile the changed economic base has had its own effects on the development of consciousness. In order to construct communism, the new human being must be forged at the same time as the material base.

The new human being. A creature stripped of fat and arrogance, who believes in the biblical statement that all people are gods; who rejects exploitation, despises superfluous objects and aims at the supreme joy, which is to forget oneself.

This is the finest utopia ever conceived in the history of Latin America: the new being. If we reach this much delayed goal, myth and reality will be, for the first time in the human adventure, a single and indivisible entity in our land. Creating this new being for the citizens of the twenty-first century will be our most valuable contribution to humanity. For we are about to overcome being dazzled by Europe, by the sophisticated and lifeless values of its culture. We are acquiring a consciousness of our identity. We are putting our own thinking into practice, without dogmatism. Every day we achieve a greater consciousness of what we are, a consciousness of our historical situation, of our limitations, and, at the same time, of our originality.

This is the pathway towards a philosophy of liberation. We have to take European tradition on board, but not hammer it in like a nail. We must assimilate its trends and techniques, but only in so far as they function to express more fully what is our own. Clearly, we have neither a philosophy nor a science which is ours, but in the realm of art and literature we have monuments, verbal, sculptural, musical, which amaze Europeans, North Americans, Africans and Asians alike. The list is enormous, and this is so because our poets, novelists and chroniclers were faithful receptors of the structures of mythical thought. They gave voice to the voices of the people.

The typical clichés of our artistic expression, spiced up for a Eurocentric public, must now be politically transformed. The response to our social problems is closely linked to acknowledgement and respect for our traditions. As our best artists and writers have done, we must have due reverence for what our myths decree, for they persist as guides in the memories of our people.

*   *   *

Our real task is liberation. The social reality of Latin America, poverty, exploitation, disempowerment, will be transformed so as to give access to our great fundamental myth: liberty. And liberty is inseparable from revolution. It is a sin against the spirit of our lands to ignore the call to revolution, the supreme act of liberty. Revolution is the conquest of our identity, the only way to preserve our tradition, our true tradition, the tradition of the people, and to achieve the same contemporaneity as the other nations on this planet.

It is said, especially in the big capitals of the west, that Latin America's revolutionary movement has been in recession since the recent changes in eastern Europe. I would say this is not the case. Quite the contrary. Despite the FSLN's negative results in the last election, the revolutionary project in Nicaragua is still alive. Despite mistaken prophecies, Cuba continues more confidently, with greater dignity and certainty than ever before. On the other hand there are spectacular changes in the correlation of power within certain countries such as Brazil and Uruguay. This does not mean that our old diseases have been cured, for in general the Left is still divided. We know only too well how incapable the majority of communist parties are of understanding the reality and originality of 'our America'. But this deficiency is being overcome by the new generations.

Mistrust, obsession with seeing recalcitrant symptoms in certain popular movements, even our own Sandinista movement, is being overtaken by the explosiveness of religious festivals. In our America we need people with imagination, critics, heretics, dreamers, not frigid ideologues nor those who chant prayers. In a word, we need revolutionaries. The reality of Latin America needs critical revolutionaries more than ever, because here the revolution will have to be critical or there will be no revolution at all.

The terrifying social reality of our continent, poverty and exploitation, has its origins in the unbridled ambition of imperialism, and the unjust international economic order which to all appearances seems to have been imposed on the world by the malign spirit, in forgetfulness of all decency. No economic programme, no distribution of money and threats can change this reality. To do so we need a radical, structural change and change of this kind is called revolution. Such a premonition, which springs from the very source of our dreams cannot be explained away by 'East-West confrontation', by 'international communist conspiracy' and similar slogans blazoned by the press agencies and the propaganda apparatus. It can only be explained by reality. Just a few figures and statistics are enough to astound.

More than 40 per cent of families in our region live in a state of poverty, and 25 per cent in a state of total destitution. At the end of the millennium, it is estimated that the numbers of those in poverty will be 250 million. In our America one out of every two of our children at the age of six is condemned to live in precarious circumstances or on public charity. More than 100 million Latin Americans show symptoms of malnutrition. Thirty per cent of the population of the continent is unemployed or under-employed. The rate of child mortality is more than 100 per 1,000 in certain areas. We depend on agriculture and mining, yet 1 per cent of the landowners own more than 60 per cent of the land in which gold is found and seeds germinate. And all this without taking into consideration the annual payment of the external debt which reaches tens of thousands of millions of dollars. To say that the external debt is unpayable and illegal is to mouth a commonplace. It is immoral – a sentence of death.

As a Nicaraguan I believe – like Garcia Márquez – in the possibility of 'a new and sweeping kind of living utopia, and not only for Latin America, where lineages condemned to a hundred years of solitude will in the end get a second and permanent chance on this earth', though Latin Americans, I would like to add, have been condemned not to 100 but to 500 years of solitude.

When the Nicaraguan Miskitos were invaded by the half-breed of Spanish stock, they called the town inhabited by the strangers Hispail town, and, so that there should be no misunderstandings, the town which they inhabited themselves they called Kipla town, which in their language is the land of human beings. Like our Miskito aboriginals we believe in the existence of human beings. We will never treat anyone like an animal – which is what the colonialists called our ancestors. We will treat all like human beings. The day when all people treat each other as equals will be the day when the miracle of revolution will have been perfected in this savage and contradictory world. We believe in humankind, even in those people who because they live in neo-colonial societies – sometimes to their own regret – continue to be our enemies. But they too, like ourselves, are subject to change.

The new human beings of Latin America, now that we have discovered them, will conquer Europe, not in order to colonise it, but in order to liberate it, so that its own mythical ceremonies can be initiated afresh, so that they can arise again from their solemn and wonderful burial ground. The citizens of those countries must be persuaded that liberty should exist not only in the vicinity of the Prado, on the banks of the Seine or the river Moskva, but should be enjoyed by all the peoples of the world.

TOMAS BORGE
Former FSLN Interior Minister

Indigenous land rights in Ecuador

As the 500th anniversary of the conquest nears, indigenous protest in the Americas is gathering momentum. In Ecuador, in June 1990, there was an uprising which brought the country to a standstill. Roads were blockaded, *haciendas* occupied and food supplies to the cities almost dried up. It lasted ten days and 600,000 indigenous people participated. At the root of the protest was the demand for land, as the key to their economic and cultural survival, and for economic and political empowerment.

The uprising was unprecedented. According to Luis Macas, leader of the country's principal Indian federation, CONAIE, it served as a 'training ground' for political mobilisation, and opened a new 'political space' for the country's four and a half million indigenous people, some 40 per cent of the total population and from eleven different Indian nations. A year later, tension is still simmering, but progress has been minimal. Negotiations with the government have ground to a halt, the military has increased its control of the countryside, taking on a new and alarming role in 'rural development', armed paramilitary guards have appeared on large estates, and terrorist attacks have occurred against the Catholic Church where it has supported indigenous claims. Land invasions and an escalating counter-offensive of evictions have brought violence, including the assassination of indigenous leaders. Land hunger is acute. Almost half the country's agricultural land is held by 1.5 per cent of landowners; 67 per cent of farmers live on less than five hectares; 25 per cent subsist on plots of less than one hectare. The majority of these are Indians.

Landowner opposition

Indigenous organisations are poised between another uprising and the struggle to manipulate existing machinery for land reform. Under the agrarian reform law, land redistribution is authorised on the grounds of failure to fulfil the productive function of the land or demographic pressure. According to an analysis of land conflicts carried out by the Quito-based Ecumenical Human Rights Commission (CEDHU), applications by peasant associations are persistently paralysed by landowner opposition. Estate owners bribe or otherwise pressure the state land reform body, IERAC, use threats and violence against applicants, and imprison leaders on false criminal charges. Where cases succeed at first instance, they are almost always overturned on appeal by an executive-appointed committee. Land is declared 'immune' from redistribution. According to Elsie Monge, president of CEDHU: 'The lack of a just and effective agrarian politics is multiplying land conflicts in the country, creating a climate of violence, abuse and arbitrary authority.'

In the Andean community of San Francisco de Cajas, for example, 400 indigenous families first made a legal claim in 1983 for lands on an estate which they have worked for generations, first under a system of legal servitude, later under mechanisms of unpaid labour in return for a share of the harvest and use of grazing lands. Death threats followed by the landowners, who are closely tied to the government, and the claim was refused. The community renewed their claim in 1989, and occupied the land. IERAC declared this an invasion and three violent police evictions followed over the course of the year, causing injuries and the death of an elderly woman. Two prominent leaders were imprisoned for nine months. Paramilitaries took up occupation of the land.

An occupation of the state congress on the first anniversary of the uprising, led by CONAIE, demanded amnesty for some 1,000 indigenous leaders imprisoned following land conflicts, and the control of paramilitary groups. Government action to provide ex post facto legalisation of the groups as private security firms is viewed as a tactic to offset accusations of death squad activity.

Empty lands

In the Amazonian region, indigenous peoples are under increasing pressure from oil companies and colonists rather than from estate owners. Colonisation laws from the 1960s have sought to relieve land hunger in the rest of the country by granting titles to so-called 'empty lands' in the rainforest. The indigenous Shuar Federation has had some success in resisting this by claiming land title in the name of Shuar communities on the basis of traditional possession. Some 75 per cent of holdings are now legalised, and leaders plan to build this up, block by block, into a territory to be held in the name of the Shuar nation.

Land title does not, however, give rights over resources in the sub-soil, which are retained by the state. Thus, the grant of territory in 1983 to the Huaorani people has been an illusory victory, as the oil companies continue to invade and destroy their lands. Nearby, under the spotlight of international ecological concern, the Yasuni National Park has been established. Indigenous peoples who have traditionally inhabited the area are permitted to remain, but in practice many have been encroached upon by oil excavation. A decision in October 1990 to ban petroleum exploitation in national parks was lifted a month later under pressure from multinational oil companies.

Military harassment is also a serious problem. In the case of the Quichua Añango community within the Yasuni park, the military has burned homes and ordered the inhabitants to leave, laying claim to the area for military training on the grounds that, as park land, it belongs to the state. This points to the serious danger that Indians will be hounded from their lands under the guise of ecological protection, while exploitation of the area proceeds unhindered.

'Nations within a nation'
The processing of land claims via narrow administrative channels masks an issue going to the heart of the nation-state. Fears of 'nations within a nation' lie behind the government's rejection of the uprising's most radical demands for land rights and a plurinational state.

The modern Latin American state is founded on the liberal conception of a unified physical, economic and juridical infrastructure and an ideology of equal rights and citizenship. The indigenous movement and a growing body of international law subverts this ideology. The movement demands recognition of indigenous peoples' collective right to self-determination as 'communities, peoples and nations' within the state, defined by their status as descendants of the original inhabitants of the area who were conquered and subordinated by a different ethnic group (ILO Convention on Indigenous and Tribal Peoples, no. 169, 1989).

The 1986 Quito declaration by the indigenous peoples of Latin America demands an end to assimilationist policies, juridical recognition of territorial rights based on prior ownership including rights to the resources of the sub-soil, and recognition of systems of self-government as a fundamental factor of self-determination. The validity of legal-political systems dating from pre-conquest times, including distinctive systems of land ownership which do not treat land as a commodity, is thus reasserted by virtue of the illegitimacy of colonial and post-colonial state control.

At the heart of these demands is the right of the group to control its own material and cultural development. In the words of the president of the Shuar Federation , Miguel Puwainchir: 'We must have a stake in the land from which to organise ourselves, to preserve and build our values and our culture.' Where the group forms an identifiable and homogeneous community, this brings claims to a specific territory, with associated political rights. Where settlement has become dispersed and the population mixed, the situation is more complex, and raises issues not of claims to a definable physical territory, but to land rights and to a distinctive legal-political voice. In both cases, powers of decision-making require linkage to broader national institutions, which must in turn relinquish a homogeneous and monopolistic view of state control.

In any country where a substantial minority or majority of the population is indigenous, or where the indigenous population is situated in key areas of natural resources, recognition of these rights would fundamentally alter the course of legitimate development. In Ecuador, faced with the opposition of the state and the oligarchy blocking progress within existing legal and political channels, the heterogeneous indigenous movement also risks defeat through exploitation of internal divisions and the fragmentation of demands. 'We are like the five fingers of one hand, all shapes and sizes, but we must close together as one fist if we are to achieve our goals', says Miguel Puwainchir. Real change can only come about with unity, but with another uprising may come a blood bath.

Quito   LISA SMITH